MAGNIFICENTLY UNREPENTANT

The Story of Merve Wilkinson and Wildwood

MAGNIFICENTLY UNREPENTANT

The Story of Merve Wilkinson and Wildwood

Goody Niosi

Heritage
House

National Library of Canada Cataloguing in Publication Data

Niosi, Goody, 1946-
    Magnificently unrepentant

    Includes index.
    ISBN 1-894384-32-6

    1. Wilkinson Merve. 2. Foresters—British Columbia—Biography.
3. Environmentalists—British Columbia—Biography. 4. Sustainable
forestry—British Columbia. I. Title.

SD129.W54N56 2001   634.9'092   C2001-911233-5

First edition 2001

Heritage House acknowledges the financial support of the
Government of Canada through the Book Publishing Industry
Development Program (BPIDP), Canada Council for the Arts, and
the British Columbia Arts Council for our publishing activities.

Cover and book design by Darlene Nickull
Edited by Terri Elderton

HERITAGE HOUSE PUBLISHING COMPANY LTD.
Unit #108 – 17665 66A Ave., Surrey, B.C. V3S 2A7

Printed in Canada

Dedication

This book is dedicated to Merve, of course, but also to all those who—like him—fight tirelessly and against great odds to preserve a green and beautiful world for all the generations to come.

Thanks

Thanks to the wonderful folks at Heritage House who made the transition from manuscript to book so effortless and so much fun: editor Terri Elderton, designer and production person Darlene Nickull, and publisher Rodger Touchie, who is such a delight to work with.

Thanks also to my friend and mentor Barry Broadfoot, and to Thora Howell, whose encouragement, faith, and support were valuable beyond measure.

And thanks to Bart for his unconditional support.

THE PAYOFF

For many years I had heard of this living legend. Now at last I was approaching him in his own habitat. I mean quite literally habitat in the sense of ecosystem. And I mean quite literally his own. The road wandered like a trail in a storybook. It was well kept and yet seemed to be from the olden days. It belonged. It was part of the majestic, mossy forest and completely unlike the slashing scars of modern forest roads. Its meandering presented vistas that delighted my artist's eyes and would even at a subliminal level bring a sense of beauty and peace to any eye ... any soul.

A pileated woodpecker called and then a Swainson's thrush. More than one winter wren challenged the forest spaces with his extended tinkling arpeggios. I expected that I would be led to Merve Wilkinson, the legend I hoped to meet, but somehow it did not matter. I found myself in a state of timelessness. I was inside a Longfellow poem, "This is the forest primeval, the murmuring pines and the hemlocks." Well, maybe not pines, but certainly cedars, firs, and hemlocks. However it did seem like the "forest primeval" and, I sensed, it always would.

Then I rounded a bend and there was a small group of attentive people dwarfed by the trees around them. They were listening to a lean and energetic man. His visage had the timelessness of the setting, but his lively movements were those of a youngster. Following his gestures, the group would gaze at the treetops then swing around and stare at the ground. This was Merve Wilkinson performing in his theatre, his forest. Scientific facts tumbled out, well layered with no-nonsense opinions. "Some tell me I'm crazy. Well, I've been crazy a lot in my life and it's paid off." As we laugh we all nod in agreement. It has not only paid off for Merve, it has paid off for nature, and as more people learn from him, it is paying off for the planet.

—Robert Bateman, May 2001

Contents

Foreword

I first met Merve at Wildwood on a coolish morning in 1988 with twenty or so of my third-year University of Victoria environmental studies students. This was when the conflict between forest companies and environmentalists on Vancouver Island was at a fever pitch over the logging of magnificent stands of old-growth temperate rain forest in such areas as Clayoquot Sound and the Carmanah Valley. The class had already been to Carmanah. On our drive there we became briefly lost in one of MacMillan Bloedel's numerous clear-cuts, guided by a makeshift map that simply said, "left at the large cedar stump." We eventually discarded the map and spent half an hour wandering through the clear-cut, which one student referred to as a "biological holocaust" and another as a "moonscape."

When we arrived at Merve Wilkinson's Wildwood, the contrast was remarkable. Here was a managed forest that still retained much of its original composition as well as the complete range of age and species types typical of an intact forest ecosystem for this area of Vancouver Island. And yet the property that year had already been logged eight times since 1945!

For two hours, Merve gave us a lesson in sustainable ecosystem-based selective forestry. Merve explained that it is possible to have a healthy environment and a sustainable forest economy—provided one deeply cares for and maintains the entire forest biotic community. Indeed, he appeared to know every tree and every family of flickers, pileated woodpeckers, eagles, brown creepers, and squirrels that use Wildwood as their home. He described how the squirrels help to regenerate the forest by planting the Douglas fir seeds and how he manipulates the canopy to allow the light to "release" shade-suppressed trees. He told us about the importance of maintaining red alder to help prevent root rot, the need to protect woodpecker populations for insect control, how roads should be designed to prevent soil erosion, and the importance of maintaining many of the largest and healthiest conifers for natural seed regeneration.

Later, when we sat in his orchard by the lake, he told us what logging was like on Vancouver Island in the 1930s, 40s, and 50s. With stories from his past, he illustrated not only the pitfalls of conventional forestry, but also how the forest industry could provide sustainable jobs and protect the environment by adopting the eco-forestry techniques he had pioneered. The students were deeply impressed by Merve and by what they had seen at Wildwood. As we prepared to leave, the whole class broke into spontaneous applause. One young woman called out, "Merve for forest minister!" And a male student asked, "Can I come again— and bring my parents?"

This was the first of many classes I've taken to see Merve Wilkinson in the last dozen years. Thanks to his generosity of time and spirit, trips to Wildwood have become an integral component of all third-year environmental studies classes at the University of Victoria. Merve is an excellent role model because he "walks the talk." He is also playing a crucial role in shaping the future of this province by showing the public, by example, the incredible things people can achieve when they dare to think outside of the box. Moreover, many of the principles Merve employs in ecosystem-based forestry can also be applied in other areas of resource usage.

In terms of forestry practices, Merve has definitely stepped beyond the conventional framework. The type of ecoforestry that Merve has helped to pioneer is not just about learning to live sustainably with whole forest ecosystems. It's also about learning to reject many of the dominant and destructive economic myths that we have all grown up with. Perhaps one reason Merve is so loved by his supporters and disliked by his opponents is that the very existence of Wildwood brings into stark relief all the problems and contradictions of the conventional corporate forestry model.

To fully appreciate what Merve has achieved, it is important to view his accomplishments in a larger social context. In late 1999, millions of television viewers were riveted to their sets as they watched thousands of anti World Trade Organization (WTO) demonstrators collide with police in the "Battle in Seattle." Nearly a year and a half later, a similar clash occurred between protesters and tear-gas-wielding police at the Free Trade Area of the Americas (FTAA) summit conference in Quebec City. These events were about more than international trade and the growing ability of corporate giants to dictate a region's future agenda or environmental and social values. They also represented the collision between very different visions for the future of our planet.

The WTO and the FTAA are embodiments of what has been called the "expansionist" world view. According to this perspective, ever-expanding human needs and wants can be satisfied through ever-expanding economic growth and resource usage. Yet all too frequently the conventional economic system destabilizes communities and destroys their local ecological systems. Advocates of this economic model rarely ask themselves whether this kind of development can be sustained indefinitely without making the world largely uninhabitable. In fact, recent ecological footprint research suggests that we would need the resources and waste absorption capacity of two additional planets if everyone in the world enjoyed a North American lifestyle.

The myth of superabundance is fast making our world ecologically untenable. This environmental crisis has been caused by:

- a fourfold population increase during the last century;

- the creation of a global economy that is marked by increasing disparities between rich and deprived regions;

- accelerating depletion of the planet's forests, ocean life, and virtually all other ecosystems upon which all species depend for survival; and

- a corresponding increase of pollution and environmental destruction in every continent.

During the 20th century, the global economy expanded twenty times, the consumption of fossil fuels grew 30-fold, and industrial production increased 50-fold. Most of this growth has taken place since 1950, and it cannot continue at this pace. Our planet has limited resources and limited waste absorption capacity. Unless we change our consumption patterns quickly, especially in the wealthy countries of the North, our planet's ecological systems will be irreversibly damaged.

We cannot create a truly viable society until we accept that the status quo will not suffice. Fortunately, the events in Seattle, Quebec City, and Genoa have shown that a growing number of people and civil society groups are beginning to embrace an emerging ecological world view that supports and encourages radical change. Like Merve, these people are committed to pioneering new, sustainable methods of resource extraction and usage that are socially just and based on community stability and maintenance of ecological integrity.

The struggle between the two perspectives—the conventional expansionist world view and the emerging ecological world view—may be likened to a young bird beginning to break out of its egg. The eggshell is our current economic system, the status quo. For so many of us it is still associated with security and comfort and the prospect of leaving it behind tends to create deep resistance. But as the cracks in the expansionist "egg" become more apparent, we can choose to either hold on to its policies and practices and hope to patch it back together, or, to identify with a very different set of ways of thinking and acting—the emerging fledgling.

Merve has consciously chosen to act as one of the midwives (or midhusbands!) for the birth of the emerging ecological world view. In doing so, he has experienced opposition, personal attack, and ridicule from people threatened by his work. His beliefs and strength of conviction have been tested time and again. Yet his pioneering work in ecoforestry has become a magnificent model and is a testament to the fact that this method of forestry can be very successful.

—Duncan M. Taylor
Professor of Environmental Studies
University of Victoria

Chapter 1

Accidental Fame

Merve Wilkinson has organized unions, berated the RCMP, written scathing letters to heads of government, and gone head-to-head with the forestry giants. He wears his 1993 sentencing for protesting clear-cutting in Clayoquot Sound like a badge of honour. The sentencing judge, after listening to Merve's defence, called him "magnificently unrepentant."

Among the awards Merve has been given are the B.C. Forests Excellence Award, the B.C. Ministry of the Environment Award, B.C. Senior Citizen of the Year, and the Cowichan Community Land Trust Stewardship Award. In 2001 he was inducted into both the Order of British Columbia and the Order of Canada.

At 88, Merve Wilkinson stands less tall and straight than he once did. Age and hip replacement surgery have taken their toll. His back is stooped from years of logging. His fingers are gnarled and curl inwards, not from arthritis but from decades of wrapping themselves around a stuttering chainsaw. But the lines on his face are permanently etched in the shape of a smile, and his eyes shine with life. They are the clear blue eyes of a young man discovering the world for the first time and delighting in what they see.

Merve lives in a unique place called Wildwood. The house that he built himself is at the end of a long drive that winds through part of his 77-acre forest. His forest is different from the surrounding woods in Yellow Point on Vancouver Island: the trees are taller, bigger, and older. The landscape is reminiscent of Germany or Switzerland. How it got to look like that is his favorite topic of conversation.

"This is a system of sustainable forestry," he says. "That means you harvest only what you grow in the forest and no more. If you ever do go over, you don't harvest again until you've rebuilt. This system is not new. Switzerland and Austria have been doing this for nearly 250 years. Germany completely banned clear-cutting in 1993."

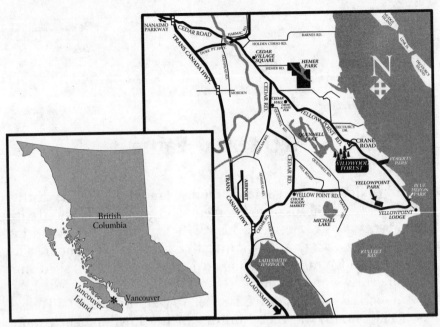

Wildwood is located on Vancouver Island just north of 49° latitude.

Merve Wilkinson was born in Nanaimo in 1913. His father was a steam engineer; his mother was a registered nurse. His parents lived in the coal miners' camp until he was almost four years old, then they moved to a large acreage on Quennell Lake in Yellow Point. Yellow Point, just south of Nanaimo on the east coast of Vancouver Island, juts out into the Strait of Georgia and laps up sunshine when the rains pelt down on the coastal range mountains of the mainland. Today the area retains its untamed charm, even though the land is dotted with working farms, smaller acreages, and even some half-acre city-sized lots. There are plenty of parks, trails, lakes, and the big trees of the temperate rain forest. But in 1915, when Merve's family came here, the pioneers were just beginning to settle the area.

"I grew up in this environment," Merve says, "and at that time all the original settlers were here. They were marvellous people. They were as different from each other as day is from night, but when it came to the community, they were not individuals—they worked together. From them, I learned the value of working with things, not against them. It was a community where people meant something to each other and where nobody ever suffered; the neighbours came to help when it was needed. That's the way community should be."

The land he grew up on and the community he lived in shaped young Merve's ideas and philosophy as surely as did his parents' work ethic. "I grew up with nature," he says, "and now I'm working with quite a few of the Aboriginal peoples, particularly the elders and the younger ones. You find that when people grow up with nature and live with nature, they have a very different attitude; they have a very different understanding of the world. I could hope that we destroy ourselves before we destroy the environment because that would be much more desirable. The earth can get along without people; we can't get along without the earth."

Merve learned respect for the land from the elders, his neighbours, and his teachers. There was one teacher in particular who had a profound influence on Merve Wilkinson's life. After he had bought this beautiful forested property, he had no idea what to do with it. He went to the University of British Columbia and decided on a course in agriculture. He had land and it seemed to make sense to farm it. The Swedish professor teaching the course steered young Wilkinson to forestry.

Unfortunately, there was no course offered in North America that the professor could recommend. But he had taken an interest in Merve. He arranged for the latest forestry course to be sent from Sweden, translated it for Merve, and put him through the course. "I wrote the final exam, the same as if I had done the course in Sweden," Merve says, "and his wife made a beautiful scroll for me. It was one in a million. He gave me the best words of advice that any man can give anybody at the end of a course: 'Don't think this has made a forester out of you; it's only given you the tools to learn to become one. Take it from there.'"

On that foundation, Merve Wilkinson worked his land. He recalls being offered $1,500 for all the timber on it. He just laughed. And he's been logging the land, a little bit at a time, all his life. Over the years, the property has provided him with two-thirds of his income. But he also explains that he has quite a high standard of living. The other one-third of his income came from building, not just with wood but also stone. The fireplace in his own home is a striking example of the magnificent stonework he has done. This home, which he shares with his wife Anne, has become a mecca for students from all over the world.

His fame (or notoriety) began in 1985. Wilkinson was watching the CBC show, *Pacific Report*. The subject of the show was the disappearance of Canada's trees. Wilkinson wrote a letter to the producer, Cam Cathcart, explaining that the forest didn't have to be lost and that there was an alternative to clear-cutting. Cathcart phoned Wilkinson, and after two-and-a-half hours on the phone, he asked permission to come over and do some filming. Merve said, "Absolutely!"

The show went on the air. "The phone started ringing ten minutes after the program was finished, and it didn't stop until midnight," says Merve. "People called from all across the province and from down in the States. That started people wanting to come and see us and teachers wanting to bring their classrooms through. So I've been teaching ever since."

If Merve is teaching any one thing, if he wants to leave one thing behind, it's that there is an alternative to clear-cutting and that clear-cutting is a disaster. But inevitably, his legacy will prove to be much broader. His work with the environment is equalled by his work with children and youths. He is a charter member of the Suzuki Foundation Council of Elders and hosts a yearly gathering of LIFE participants at his Wildwood forest. LIFE stands for Leadership Initiative for Earth. Since 1995, LIFE sailing ships have served as an educational and training ground for youths aged thirteen to eighteen. Elders are an integral part of the flotillas that sail the Strait of Georgia. Jane Goodall, Jean-Michel Cousteau, and Robert Bateman have all been elders on LIFE trips.

On March 27, 1999, the first tree to be used in building the Lifeship 2000 was felled on Merve Wilkinson's land. The Lifeship 2000 project was intended to extend the LIFE program to cover the globe. Youths and elders were to travel the world on the Lifeship 2000, spreading a message of peace, unity, and environmental awareness. Government funding for the project fell through, and the ship was never completed.

But the felling of the first tree at Wildwood was symbolic of the philosophy behind LIFE and the Lifeship 2000. A group of youths, members of LIFE, blessed the tree before it was felled:

I have listened to the voice of time and have heard the elements sing–and now I know that my spirit will pass on. It will glide through the waters and fly with the wind–and follow the path of the stars. The end of my life will lead to the beginnings of others. My spirit will travel on: the cycle complete and within the future again, we all will meet.

When his time comes, it may be an apt blessing for Merve Wilkinson as well.

Chapter 2

Family Roots

Since the divorce, Merve Wilkinson had gotten into the habit of watching television while he did the supper dishes. His favourite show was the CBC's *Pacific Report*, hosted and directed by Cam Cathcart. More often than not, the topics and people on the show were interesting and the material was presented intelligently.

On this particular warm spring night, while the sun was setting and sending orange ripples over the lake outside the kitchen door, Merve listened to the mayor of Fort St. John in northern British Columbia bewail his region's dying forest industry.

"What are we going to do when the timber vanishes?" he asked.

I listened to this guy's wails. He was a good enough mayor probably, but when it came to forestry he was as far off the track as a locomotive is when it's being built.

By the time the program ended Merve had a head of steam on. He pulled a chair up to the kitchen table and wrote an impassioned letter to Cam Cathcart.

"This man should learn something about forestry before he gets on the air with this kind of uninformed talk," Merve wrote. "It's not necessary for B.C. to run out of timber. We are going to if we persist in doing what the Fort St. John mayor thinks we should do."

Then Merve outlined his own practice of sustainable forestry at Wildwood, his 77-acre parcel of land in Yellow Point.

When Merve's letter hit his desk, Cathcart picked up the phone.

I was glad he was paying the phone bill. He phoned me at 10:30 in the morning and we talked until about noon.

What had Merve been doing in his forest? Was it working? Could it work on a broader scale? And lastly, Cathcart asked, "Can I come and film your operation?"

"Sure," Merve said. "I'd be delighted."

A week later, a camera crew arrived from Vancouver. Merve Wilkinson was ready for stardom—he even had the looks to carry it off. Like his father, Merve was lean and tall. His body was hard. He stood straight. His smile split his face in two and showed a double row of teeth a film idol would envy. His eyes danced. Best of all, he liked the attention and he embraced the opportunity to tell the world about sustainable forestry.

Two weeks later the program hit the air and Merve's life changed forever.

The show ended at 7:30 p.m. and Merve's phone didn't stop ringing until the wee hours of the morning. People called from Oregon and Washington State and Wisconsin and from all over Canada. Was this kind of forestry real? Was it possible?

Merve's answer was then, as it is now, simple: Yes it's possible—and if we are to save our forests for future generations, it is the only sort of forestry that is viable on our planet today.

Since the day the program aired, Merve's home that he christened Wildwood has been a centre for education that attracts people from all over the world, and Merve has found himself at the storm centre of conflict with a large segment of North America's forest industry. But controversy has never bothered him. Truth is, he takes a certain amount of gleeful pride in generating it and then meeting his battles head-on. In all likelihood, he was born confident, strong, and ready to fight for what he believes in.

Merve Wilkinson was born on September 22, 1913, at 2:30 a.m. He weighed in at twelve pounds, and Christina Wilkinson never had another baby. Neither she nor her husband William wanted to go through that experience again. So Merve grew up as an only child. But he wasn't lonely. Merve was born into a community that was close-knit, where people were in and out of each other's houses and where neighbours looked after each other. There was never a lack of playmates or of adult role models either.

The people around him as he grew up took a straightforward and practical approach to life. From them he learned to value his mind and to make decisions based on reasoning and logic. Merve was never a sentimentalist; indeed, he was quite the opposite. He would never hesitate to shoot a deer if he was hungry, or to put a bullet between the eyes of a pet if it was ill. Merve grew up with both feet planted firmly on the ground, never letting his emotions run away with him, and indeed, his tranquil boyhood gave him little cause to experience emotional trauma. He also grew up with a strong moral sense of right and wrong—so strong that never in his life did he doubt or question the correct path to take. It was perhaps his sense of righteousness more than anything else that carried him through his battles and conflicts.

But the story of Merve Wilkinson's life begins long before he was born. To understand the kind of man he is, you have to look at his heritage: the coal miner, the veterinarian, the sharpshooter, the rebel, the Methodist minister, and the musician all left their imprints as surely as did his genes.

Christina and William Wilkinson lived in Nanaimo near the South Wellington mine. At that time Nanaimo was well-known as a mining town with five or six active mines in the area. William was a steam engineer and worked part-time in the power plant as a stationary engineer. He also drove the locomotive up and down the ten miles of track from the mine in South Wellington to the ships at Boat Harbour. Although he worked above ground and although he had tried his hand in a retail business venture, William had ended up following an old family mining tradition.

William's family came from Carlisle in the Cumbria district of northern England, where they had a long history of going down into the mines. With few exceptions, the pits and mines throughout Europe at that time had brutal working conditions. The casualty rates were high. Individuals, both good and bad, owned the mines. Good owners were rare, and jobs with them were scarce simply because every miner in Europe wanted to work for such a man. The bad owners were very bad indeed and to go against them usually meant trouble.

Robert Wilkinson—William's father and Merve's grandfather—immigrated to Canada in 1889 because he was blacklisted by the notorious cartel of coal barons who wielded significant political clout in England. In his time, Bob Wilkinson, also a Methodist lay minister, was a revolutionary. He advocated getting children under the age of twelve out of the mines. He also lobbied for a ten-hour workday and a six-day workweek. At the time children were down in the mines twelve hours a day, seven days a week. Tory rhetoric labelled Bob Wilkinson a communist. Not one to shy away, Wilkinson wore the brand proudly. "The communist of today is the conservative of tomorrow," he responded.

He was so right. You can be very radical right now, but many years from now what you were radical about has been accomplished and somebody else is being radical and you're just being conservative. I've always thought there was more wisdom in that than met the eye.

But his "communist" label wasn't the only reason Bob Wilkinson was blacklisted. Since time immemorial, the Conservatives had held the riding he lived and worked in. Bob and his friends were instrumental in expelling the Conservative incumbent and electing the Cumbria riding's first Liberal representative.

Being ousted from the mines wasn't a huge setback for Bob Wilkinson. He'd been putting money aside for years. With those savings and the few pounds his friends lent him, he paid for a passage to Canada for himself, his wife Annie, and his three-year-old son William aboard the SS *Ascania*.

The trip from England to Canada aboard the old Cunard liner was the stormiest passage the *Ascania* had ever experienced. It took an extra day and a half to reach Halifax. During one storm a window in the wheelhouse was broken by a 120-foot wave.

There were only three people on the ship who weren't seasick: the captain, the chief engineer, and three-year-old William Wilkinson. With little William's parents under the weather, the Captain wisely took the lad up to his cabin where he could keep an eye on him. Meanwhile, the mate and some of the boiler crew were functioning just enough to keep the ship going. The earliest picture Merve had of his dad shows him arriving in Halifax, coming down the gangplank holding the Captain's hand.

Once he'd recovered from the journey, Bob Wilkinson decided he was not impressed with the coal mining in Nova Scotia and prepared his family for the long trek across Canada. He'd heard good things about the mining business in British Columbia, so the Wilkinson family headed west on the Canadian Pacific Railway. They arrived in Nanaimo in 1889.

Bob was a good miner and landed work right away. There were several good mine managers in Nanaimo. There were some poor ones, too. The way grandson Merve heard it, the Dunsmuir father and son were the worst, and Samuel Robins was the best.

Robert Dunsmuir had spent twenty years ruthlessly building his fortune on the backs of the miners. He died the same year that Bob Wilkinson reached Nanaimo, and it was left to his son James to act as the oppressive foil to the kindly Sam Robins.

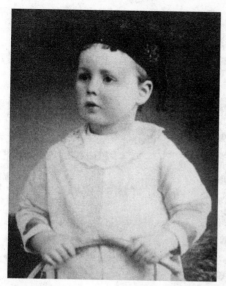 

Merve's father, William Wilkinson,
as a young child of four and as a young man.

Robins managed the Canadian Collieries Mine on the Nanaimo waterfront. He had a policy that if you arrived in Nanaimo with any talent to offer, he'd find you a job. B.C. was a young province and Nanaimo a growing town that needed good people. If you were a musician or a good tradesman—if you had any skill to bring to his town—Robins would help get you settled in and gainfully employed.

> *If it could be said that anyone built Nanaimo, it was Sam Robins.*
> *It was a town in which no one went without because everybody was*
> *concerned about their neighbour. Somehow or other, you would be*
> *looked after. People concerned themselves with abiding by the law so*
> *there was no crime. They were interested in and supported all the*
> *"good endeavours": choirs, bands, local athletes …*

Robins' philosophy was simple and sensible: Nanaimo had good coal that was attracting good miners. They were getting a fair price for the coal and the ingredients were there to build a community. His attitude spread to the other mines. If the other owners ran too poor a show, the good miners would up and leave and hitch up with Robins.

Once Bob Wilkinson was pretty well established in Nanaimo, his brothers Tom and George came to join him from England, and then their father made the trip across the Atlantic Ocean to Canada

Merve's great-grandparents John and Anne Wilkinson. John followed in his son Robert's footsteps and came to Nanaimo to work as a watchman in the mines.

in 1894 at age 80. John, Merve's great-grandfather, took a job with the mine as the night watchman, which was the ideal situation for him. It gave him all day to go fishing, putter around, and do whatever he wanted. He finally retired at age 85.

Merve traces his distaff heritage back to his Scottish great-grandfather, a McOuat, one of the last of the Highlanders driven out of his homeland by the English. He brought his family, including sons Richard and Stuart, to Canada and settled in the Eastern Townships of Quebec. He and Richard were both veterinarians.

Stuart McOuat, Merve's grandfather, had a great empathy for the French Canadians. He spoke fluent French and eventually moved from the Scots/Irish enclave of the Eastern Townships to the outskirts of Montreal, where he married a French Canadian girl, Christina De Lalande.

Most of the McOuats migrated west in the late 1800s and early 1900s, including Stuart's son Walter and his daughter—also called Christina—who had graduated as a nurse before heading west. Christina, a musical child, had studied piano and played it marvellously. After she married Merve's father and they moved to Vancouver, she played in the Pantages Orchestra and accompanied stars like Enrico Caruso and Harry Lauder when they came on tour.

Christina's brother, Walter McOuat became a timber cruiser in B.C. and would ultimately have a strong influence on his nephew Merve's upbringing. Merve recalls his Uncle Walter had good tales to tell, especially about the bears he encountered.

He had several occasions to shoot a bear in the cookhouse of the logging camp. No one else had what it took to go into the room with a bear and shoot it. They were all too scared. So he'd go in and shoot it, and he was a dead shot. Basically, he liked bears. He said the secret was to let the bear know you're there. Don't take him by surprise. If the bear knew you were coming, he'd stick around if he wanted to see you. If he didn't want to see you, he'd get out of there. A curious bear would never hurt you. He'd just be curious. He wanted to see what you were made of. He'd smell you and have a good look at you and he'd amble away.

William Wilkinson and Christina McOuat met in Cumberland, a small community on Vancouver Island just south of Courtenay. Christina was head nurse at the hospital. William had come north from Nanaimo to Cumberland to work for the Simon Leiser Company, a small, locally owned grocery chain.

Christina and William were about 21 when they met. Merve suspects they met on the tennis court. "They were both avid players and the hospital had its own courts," Merve recalls. So they found themselves playing tennis, then they started dating. Some of those dates were hunting dates. Christina was a good shot and so was William. They both loved music. William played the clarinet and violin. Among the mining crowd in Cumberland, William and Christina were considered intellectuals. They were musical; they liked amateur theatrics and were part of the artistic crowd.

When Simon Leiser sold his business, William got a job as conductor on the small local railway that ran from Cumberland to the loading wharves of Union Bay. In those days there was no highway running up and down the east coast of Vancouver Island. To get to Cumberland, you took a boat to Union Bay and then boarded the passenger car on the coal train to Cumberland. At a top speed of ten miles per hour, it was a two- or three-hour trip.

But it was quite a relaxing thing to ride on that train. People went down in the summertime because there were lovely beaches at Union Bay. They'd go down—whole families—and have a picnic on the beach and come back when the train was done unloading its coal.

Ships waiting to load Cumberland coal at the docks at Union Bay.

They'd have time to have lunch while the train unloaded. Then they'd toot the whistle when the train was ready to head back and everybody would come back and go home. Life then was much more relaxed and much less organized, but also better organized in many ways.

Christina and William were married in Ladysmith, a small town just south of Nanaimo, on October 21, 1907, by William's father. Bob had been ordained by then because there were so few ministers in Nanaimo and he felt an obligation to fill the need. Besides himself there was only an Anglican priest who was overwhelmed by the amount of work he had to do, and a Catholic priest, Father Ryan, whose diocese was the whole of Vancouver Island. Father Ryan managed to look in on Nanaimo every three weeks.

Father Ryan and Bob Wilkinson built a wonderful if unorthodox relationship. They came up with an interdenominational arrangement that was unauthorized and quite unknown to either the Catholic or Methodist churches. Bob Wilkinson held Sunday prayer and choral services that were open to both Methodists and Catholics. On Sundays when Father Ryan was in town, Bob Wilkinson slipped off to preach elsewhere while Father Ryan performed the interdenominational service. Later, Father Ryan saw his Catholic flock privately to perform church offices. Both men recognized the value in each other. Bob Wilkinson told anyone who would listen that he had rarely met a man more sincere than Father Ryan. "And who am I to say that he is wrong and I am right?"

Merve speculates that Father Ryan probably said the same thing about Wilkinson.

After Christina and William were married, they moved to Vancouver to open a convenience store in the 600 block of East Broadway in Vancouver. They ran the shop and had their apartment on the ground floor. They rented the suite on the second floor. That was their day job. At night they played for the Pantages Orchestra. In 1912 they gave it up. They could take on so much work for only so long. Although William was only 26, his health was failing from a condition diagnosed as stress.

William's brother Jack was working at the Pacific Coast Collieries in Nanaimo. He introduced William to Samuel Robins, by then retired almost a decade but still prominent in Nanaimo. Robins helped William land a job. The big excitement at the time was steam power. The steam engine was being used more and more. William was fascinated with railroads and steam locomotives, and the South Wellington Mine had both.

As luck would have it, William had a chance to sign on as a fireman on the locomotive. His ambition was to become a steam engineer. To get there, he had to put in a certain number of hours on the boiler under the direction of a top qualified engineer. He started firing with Dick Bowlsbey, an excellent engineer who chose to work on an undistinguished, ten-mile railway because he wanted to go home to his family every night.

William learned from the best. When he'd been firing for a year, Bowlsbey said to him, "Come on, write your ticket. Why not? Then, if something happens to me, there'll be a back-up engineer. We can always get someone else to fire the thing."

William agreed and got his fourth-class engineering papers. Since he'd also been pinch-hitting in the boiler plant, he went for both stationary and rail engineering. But he was also an astute man. He knew that mines only lasted so long. His was not a job people retired on. When he got a chance to live in what had been a construction shed on the company's property, he jumped at it. At a rent of eight dollars a month, he couldn't go wrong. William and his brother

A steam engine similar to the one William Wilkinson drove.

Jack were both pretty good carpenters and they turned the shed into a cozy, comfortable, three-room cottage.

Christina and William brought their son home to that cottage. They didn't mind that it was a humble place that still looked like an ordinary shed from the outside. Christina and William wanted their own property, and they knew that the grander the house, the higher the rent and the longer it would take them to get their own place. They weren't out to impress people either. They were confident individuals who didn't need approval.

What the cabin lacked in exterior beauty, it made up for in interior comfort. Christina liked nice things. She had plenty of pictures and hangings for the walls and throws for the chesterfield. She had a big family who gave the young couple many pretty and comfortable furnishings for their home.

Their baby didn't lack either. Merve, christened William Armstrong Mervyn Wilkinson, had plenty of all the usual things to

Number One mine in Nanaimo Harbour was on strike from
1912 to 1914. It would survive until 1950, when its closure
signalled the end of the industry on Vancouver Island.

chew on, suck on, and spit out. He was a much loved and well-cared-for baby.

In 1913, when he was born, the Nanaimo miner's strike had been on for a year. The bitter strike had begun in September 1912 and lasted two years, with unrest spreading from Cumberland and Ladysmith to all the island mines.

The mine William worked for, Pacific Coast Colleries was one of two mines in the area that was not on strike for the duration. Although Pacific Coast shut down for some time, the mine was operational again by the summer of 1914.

As the situation became more desperate for many strikers, the miners at Pacific Coast decided to contribute either a full or a half-day's pay per week, according to ability, to the striking miners' fund. It was well understood that they did what they could to help their neighbours and no one who received help had to feel indebted.

The Pacific Coast Collieries works at South Wellington, circa 1910,
were connected by seven miles of track that ran along the south
shore of Holden Lake to storage bunkers at Boat Harbour.

At that time a sporadic information picket line went up in front
of the Pacific Coast mine. The picketers were there to remind them
there was a strike happening on Vancouver Island and that workers'
support for the strikers was important. The picketers didn't want to
stop anyone from going to or from the mine. It was an arrangement
everyone was pretty content with—everybody, that is, except a man
called Louis Luenthal.

Louis Luenthal had been hired by the American mining people
to organize the strike on Vancouver Island. Details didn't come to
light until years after the strike was over, but the fact was that the
American collieries were after the coal contract with the U.S. Navy.
Vancouver Island coal was far superior and the Navy had been using
it for years. The high quality of coal meant the ships could carry
less tonnage and more ammunition in its place. The American mines
could get the Navy contract only if the Vancouver Island mines
stopped producing and broke their contracts. It was Louis Luenthal's
job to make sure the Vancouver Island mines broke their contracts.
He was later rewarded for his success with the job of manager at the
Chehalis Mine in Washington State, even though he didn't know
the first thing about managing a mine.

A barquentine and a freighter coal up at Nanaimo Harbour, circa 1912.

On this particular day, when Merve was eighteen months old, the information picket line was up on the trail that ran from the mine to the post office in town. Christina and William lived on the mine side of the picket line and Christina made the trip to town almost daily, pushing Merve along in the baby carriage. Two men by the name of Unsworth and Manson were manning the picket line on this fine autumn day. Unsworth and Christina knew each other quite well. They played in the orchestra together and often enjoyed a nice chat on her way to town. But despite the friendly relations, Christina was well aware that American rabble-rousers had come to town and had taken to slipping her Colt .32 pistol under baby Merve's pillow.

On this day, Louis Luenthal had decided that the picketers should act with more authority and stop the friendly chitchat. He was standing right in the middle of the trail when Christina came along, pushing her baby carriage. It was a narrow trail with a drop-off on either side. Luenthal was an uncommonly large man and Christina had no way of getting around him.

"Where do you think you're going, Mrs. Wilkinson?" Luenthal asked.

"I'm going to the post office," Christina said.

"I don't think you are, Mrs. Wilkinson, this is a picket line."

So Christina reached over and slipped her hand under the baby's pillow. When her hand reappeared, she was twirling a Colt .32 on her finger. "Step aside, Mr. Luenthal," she said. "I'm going to the post office." Considering her formidable reputation as a crack shot, there was little doubt in anyone's mind that Christina would and could put a bullet through Luenthal's shoe without even injuring his foot.

As Unsworth told the story later, "For a man his size, Luenthal's motions were remarkable." He was off the trail before Christina had a chance to level her pistol at him. She carried on with her trip to the post office and had no more trouble after that.

Merve Wilkinson grew up in the tiny miner's cottage until he was almost four years old. The Wilkinsons had saved up enough money to buy their own property by then, but shortly before the family moved to the shores of Quennell Lake in Yellow Point, one of the greatest mining tragedies in Vancouver Island history struck the Pacific Coast mine.

The original owners had sold out to a group in New York. The new owners were interested in only two things: cutting costs and making profits. The miners had been working on a seam that was heading in the direction of an abandoned and flooded coal mine. There were no accurate mining records kept in those days, so the old owners had taken serious precautions to prevent the miners from breaking through to the old mine.

The old mine manager, who was an engineer, had had a diamond drill going up and down the face of the seam, drilling holes 150 feet ahead of the miners. If they punched through with the drill, the water would pour in the 1.5-foot-diameter hole. An over-capacity pump that could handle the water coming through the small hole was always ready to go into immediate operation. The manager knew the amount of pressure to expect and what it would take to handle it.

When new management took over, their attitude was, "Oh to hell with it, we don't need that pump down there with a pump man to operate it." They got rid of the diamond drill, too. A breakthrough was inevitable. When the miners broke into the old abandoned and flooded mine, they broke through a 50-foot wall. Fifty-five men, including some of the best miners on Vancouver Island, drowned in that accident.

The South Wellington flood never should have happened, but there was no legislation forcing mine owners to take precautions. Nanaimo—the orphans, the widows, the friends, and co-workers—mourned its loss. Resentment towards absentee owners was widespread.

Shortly after the tragedy, William Wilkinson was presented with an opportunity to move from the boiler room at the South Wellington operation to Boat Harbour, the terminus of the coal train. The engineer at Boat Harbour had decided to retire. William had his third-class papers by then and was next in line for the job. He had also been trained as an accountant, and the position at Boat Harbour required the engineer to keep records of tonnage and prices. William had the ideal qualifications for the job.

But shortly after he took the job of chief engineer, another duty was added to the job: dredging the slack coal. Slack coal, the fragments that gathered on the shipping dock, were often stored underwater to prevent spontaneous combustion. Despite precautions, slack coal fires were common for years. As soon as the coal came under fourteen feet of depth pressure, it would heat up enough to combust. The smell of coal fires in abandoned mines was carried on the air for miles around Nanaimo. It wasn't just a pollutant; it was a great waste of potential energy. Slack coal, once considered useless, could bring in some revenue if it could be pulverized.

The Pacific Coast mine engineer had applied to the federal government and got permission to use the deep tidal lagoon at Boat Harbour for storage. The lagoon was covered by water twice a day, and it didn't contain a lot of shellfish because of its depth, so he didn't see a lot of hazard in the plan. By the time they figured out how to use pulverized coal, there were 500 tons of slack coal stored in the lagoon in as good a condition as the day it came out of the mine.

Getting the slack coal out of the lagoon and ready for shipping became William's responsibility while a new clerk took over the accounting end of the business. The dredged coal was sifted through a screen to remove rocks and other foreign objects. Then they ran it into a bunker suspended over the ocean so that the salt water could drain back into the sea without harming the environment. After the mine finally shut down, the dredging operation continued for another five years.

The setting in South Wellington, where Merve first played,
was a far cry from the forest lands of Cedar.

Meanwhile, Christina and William had bought their property at Yellow Point, a rural area just south of Nanaimo that jutted out into the Strait of Georgia. Yellow Point was rich in wildlife and sparsely populated. The Wilkinson property was uncleared, but Christina didn't mind the idea of living in the woods. In fact, like her husband, she enjoyed it. William had hunted and fished in the area, and met many of the local people. He had found their new home one day while he was duck hunting with his friend Dick Bowlsbey. They were out in a small boat when they came upon a pretty bay and a charming piece of land. They looked up Mr. Simpson, the man who owned it, and found he was quite willing to sell a few acres.

The piece William marked off was thirteen-and-a-half acres. It was good lakefront land with a nice house site, plenty of water, a fine garden area, and grouse and deer in the backyard. He bought it for about $650.

Building a house was easy then. There weren't a lot of rules and regulations and hassles with subdividing. William arranged for a right of way through Simpson's land over an old track. Then he got the lumber for his house, tied it into a raft, and floated it down the lake when the wind was blowing in the right direction. He built a simple house. It was about 16 feet by 32 feet and required only two

The house where Merve grew up on the shores of Quennell Lake.

or three work bees to complete. The house had three rooms, with a wing on the side that was used as a pantry for many years. Eventually it became an indoor bathroom.

Growing up on the lake had its joys and its hazards. Merve almost drowned himself several times before he finally learned to swim. He also discovered the forest.

Even right from the start, I really had no great fear of the woods or the creatures in it and so I found myself playing with a cougar kitten very shortly after we arrived here. I was four years old and playing in the back yard right up against the forest's edge. Dad had had a big tree cut down, but there was a big chunk of it that hadn't been sawed up for wood yet. I remember that log being as high as the ceiling. It couldn't have been more than three feet, but I was a little guy and that was a pretty big object. It must have been about twenty feet long.

All of a sudden I became aware of what I thought was the neighbour's cat, looking at me from one end of the log. So I went roaring over calling, "Here, kitty, kitty." I got there and there was no sign of it, so I looked all over and there it was, peeking at me from the other end of the log. I beetled back down to the other end and off it went. We were playing hide-and-seek.

When Merve's mother looked out the window and saw what was going on, she came roaring out of the house brandishing a broom and hollering "like a banshee." Merve's playmate disappeared along with his mother and littermates. Christina hauled Merve back into the house and wouldn't let him out for an entire day.

I was mad. Oh God, I was mad at her. It was one of the few times in my life I was ever really mad at my mom. I was fit to be tied. She had spoiled my hide-and-seek game.

The next day Merve went off into the woods, looking for his cougar kitten. He didn't find the kitten, but he wandered far enough to get thoroughly lost. When Christina found her son, he was peering through the trees calling, "Here, kitty, kitty, kitty."

A long time afterwards, Merve realized that the rock on the hill overlooking the yard was an ideal place for a well-fed cougar mother to sun herself and watch her kittens at play.

That was a lesson that I didn't pick up the meaning of for a long, long time. When men and animals live in close proximity, as long as the animals are well fed and not hungry or stressed, a tremendous amount of interrelationship can take place. I've seen it so many times since, where one species will get along with another when they're normally competitive. I've had cougars and bears following me and they've been so close that when I've turned back, their tracks were filling with water. But you don't see them because the minute you turn back, they're gone. They never bothered me—they were just curious.

Chapter 3

Growing up in Yellow Point

Merve Wilkinson grew up in a community whose social life revolved around Quennell Lake. There were few roads and those were generally in poor repair, so rowboats were often the preferred method of transportation.

Residents could hop into a rowboat, or powerboat if they were lucky enough to have one, and be at their neighbour's house in a matter of minutes. Trips back and forth across the lake were frequent. They went to pay a call, to attend a party, to borrow something, or to give back something their neighbour had lent them.

People shared what they had: tools, implements, even draft horses. If a man had a lame horse, the next-door neighbour would put his horse on the man's team and they'd go to work. There were plenty of resources to work with in this new land. No one did financial planning; no one knew how their lives would work out and it didn't worry them one bit. They were busy carving a homestead out of the forest with tools they had made themselves. They raised their own crops, harvested them, and used them as their main source of food. They spun their own wool. They did what they had to do to survive and they helped each other out in the process.

There were about 25 or 30 families living in the entire Yellow Point area. They'd come from Germany, Ireland, England, the United States, Italy ... it was a rich hodgepodge of nationalities. They were people who had what it took to become pioneers in a new country. This diverse community that was Yellow Point at the turn of the century didn't happen by accident. It came about through the efforts of Robert Stevenson. He was the Crown's representative, which meant that he performed the duties of sheriff, police officer, and judge. He was responsible to the governor of British Columbia.

According to all accounts, Robert Stevenson was an upstanding man of fine character. He had all the virtues: integrity, honesty, a sense of fair play and decency. Stevenson recognized that this was a growing country and that if the government brought in good people, it had an excellent chance of becoming an even better country. Stevenson had his own project that was designed to make Nanaimo and the surrounding area a "good" country. The project involved a rather unorthodox way of populating the area.

Ships from all over the world steamed into Nanaimo harbour to load up on coal. Word had spread quickly that if you wanted to start a new life, Nanaimo was the place to do it. The local people were sympathetic and willing to help out. Some of the captains on the ships that docked in Nanaimo were fine fellows who hired good crews and treated them well; very few of those men ever jumped ship. But some crews had miserable captains. Good men on those crews couldn't wait to get off that ship, so when a ship came in captained by a less than admirable man, one or two of the crew almost always stayed behind. Often it was one of the key men—a sailmaker or a first-class carpenter or a blacksmith—who disappeared the minute he got leave to go ashore.

The man would head for the countryside, often to Yellow Point, hoping to find work, and would wind up at somebody's farm. Meanwhile, the captain would go steaming up to the government agent's office to report that a crew member was missing. Stevenson would sit down and chat with the captain and size him up. Then he'd ask in detail what the missing man was like. What did he do? What did he look like? What sort of character did he have? Then he'd say, "Thank you, captain. Your ship is leaving when?"

"Oh, we'll be coaled by Friday."

"Then you'll be clearing about Saturday?"

"Yes."

"Oh fine, thank you. I'll see what I can do for you."

After the door closed on the disgruntled captain, Stevenson would put on his hat, pick up his walking stick, and head for the main street. He'd walk up and down, meeting and greeting people who'd come in from the country to do their shopping. He knew them all by name, of course.

"Oh, by the way, John, have you seen a man by this description?" Stevenson would give him the information he'd just gleaned from the captain.

To reach their jobs at the Protection Island coal mine,
men had to travel by scow across Nanaimo Harbour.

"Yes, I think I have. What nationality is he?"

"He's Italian."

"Yes, he's over at my next-door neighbour's place."

"And you've seen him?"

"Yes."

"What's he like? Is he a likeable chap?"

"Yes, he's very pleasant. We didn't know he was off the ship,
but anyway, he's very nice."

"What do the neighbours think of him?"

"They're really happy. He's very helpful, polite, and courteous.
He amuses the kids by tying sailor's knots for them ... yes, they
think he's great."

"Would you like him as a neighbour?"

"I wouldn't mind him as a neighbour ... no, not at all. He seems
a really nice fellow. I was quite impressed."

"Okay. Tell him the ship is leaving on Saturday. If he wants to
drop by my office, say next Tuesday or Wednesday, we'll talk about
landed status."

And that's how almost half the population of Yellow Point came
to be. Every single one of them was a good citizen, Merve recalls.
Some of them were outstanding. They were good neighbours and
good friends. They brought the best of their customs with them.
They never forced them on others, but they weren't reticent about

sharing them either. If you went to a German house for dinner, you were served good, hearty German food. If you went to an Irish house, you got the Irish version of a good meal. The rest of the pioneers who settled in Yellow Point were coal miners like the Wilkinsons, who had emigrated in hopes of starting new lives in a new country. These people really cared about their community. There wasn't a get-rich-quick schemer or a land speculator in the lot.

> *When I was a boy, the old mining section of town was a delight to walk through on a spring or summer day. All the miners used canaries as a safety measure, so every house had its canary. And if you walked down Victoria Road or Nicol Street or Haliburton Avenue in the afternoon with all the birds out on the porches, there was a chorus of song all up and down the street. And the variety of gardens would almost make your head swim. Some had roses, somebody else liked nasturtiums, somebody else liked another kind of annual—there was a huge variety. The back yards would vary according to the tastes of the person and the vegetables they liked. It was a really lovely and peaceful community.*

Merve spent more time on the lake than he did in town. That was generally fine with him, although there was that night the Quennells threw a party. It was a cool November evening. The Quennells lived at the far end of the lake. William Wilkinson had a powerboat by then and they made the trip in less than half an hour. The party broke up at about midnight. William, Christina, and Merve headed back down to the makeshift dock that consisted of two big logs lashed together. There were no planks on top of the logs. Half-asleep and unaware, Merve slipped between the two logs into the icy November water.

> *I got thoroughly soused. Of course I was immediately pulled out and they peeled my clothes off and wrapped a blanket around me. I can remember saying, "I don't like it, I don't like it" all the way home. I must have sounded like a record player with a stuck needle.*

Merve grew up with the neighbourhood kids. The men made trails through the woods that connected their houses. They were good, walkable trails that allowed the women and children to visit back and forth. People didn't drop in on each other—even the children made arrangements in advance. But when they did go to visit, they spent the entire day and didn't go home until after dinner.

Each week a different household hosted a pack of the neighbourhood children. There were always enough to play hide-and-seek and if there was new hay in the barn, then that was heaven indeed. Nothing could beat the thrill of climbing up into the rafters of those great old pole-and-timber barns and hurtling down into the hay below.

But it wasn't all play. Adults and children alike believed that you ought to be helpful.

Whoever's house you were at, he would say. " Okay, you kids, I've got a job for you."

"Yes, Mr. Thomas. What do you want us to do?"

"Take my dog and go and bring the cows up from the field and put them in the barn for me."

Of course that was a big thrill, so we'd run off through the bush with the dog. The dog knew exactly what he was supposed to do. We didn't. Lots of times the dog knew more than we did. So we'd round up the cows and sometimes we'd find a new calf and that was a big thrill. Then, of course, we couldn't get that cow home and we'd go back and say, "There's a cow that's had a calf."

And he'd say, "That's early. I wasn't expecting it until tomorrow. Where's it at?"

"Come on, we'll show you."

And we'd go. Mr. Thomas would carry the calf home, and the cow would follow, and everything was fine.

Country kids had their own animals, too. Some had rabbits and some had chickens. They raised them, and when they sold them for meat, they kept the money they made on the transaction. Merve had chickens and sold the eggs.

In the summer the older kids, boys and girls of sixteen or so, took the younger ones to the beach to fish. In the spring the children walked through the woods to see how many birds' nests they could find. They knew not to disturb the nests, but the game was to find them and see if there were eggs or tiny chicks inside.

Young Bill Miles used to visit his grandfather, William Thomas, every summer. Bill's parents lived in Vancouver. A summer on Quennell Lake with his friend Merve was pure bliss. Bill and Merve got up to all sorts of things, but for sheer enjoyment, nothing could beat fishing. There was just something about feeling that tug on the end of the line and reeling in a fighting mad trout. So one fine summer's day, Bill and Merve, fishing poles in hand, set out for a favourite spot on the lake. On the way, they came across a large trout in a pool just by the outlet of the lake. While that stretch of water had run dry, the trout had stayed in the pool. Well, Bill liked to fish and there was this fine-looking trout just waiting to be caught, so Bill got his line and tossed it in. The fish wouldn't bite. The pool was only a foot deep, twelve feet long, and four feet wide. "Let's catch it," Bill said.

Well, that was an experience. We both ended up falling flat on our faces. We both got wet. We both got slimy. We finally did catch that trout, but it took us two and a half hours. How we caught it is that we got the water so muddy that eventually it couldn't see us and it couldn't see where it was going so it sort of beached itself. I pretty well threw myself on top of the fish and it slid up past my ear onto the shore. That's where Bill got it. I never worked so hard for three pounds of fish in my whole life.

Merve was six when he started school. The old East Cedar School at Yellow Point Road and DeCourcy was still in operation. It was a one-room schoolhouse with a big desk for the teacher and twenty smaller desks for the students. Eleven children went to the East Cedar School.

The school was a two-mile walk for Merve. Christina started her son off on his first day by walking him through their right of way over the Simpsons' land to Yellow Point Road. Then, pointing him north, she let him go. Sometimes she met him at the same spot on his way home.

The Simpsons were good friends by now, and Mr. Simpson, having been a schoolteacher himself, took a keen interest in young Merve's education. He always wanted to know what was going on in the school and whether young Merve was being properly taught. He liked to quiz Merve, and his little impromptu tests kept the boy alert. Merve didn't mind one bit. In fact, he made it a point to stop and chat with him in his garden or his field on his way home in the afternoons.

Merve's first year at East Cedar was uneventful. When you knew everybody at the school, there was very little to fear. There were no strangers to meet, none except the teacher and she turned out to be no threat at all. Miss Devlin was bright and breezy and related well to the children. She was strict, but the rules weren't carved in stone. But Miss Devlin left and was replaced in Merve's second year by

Miss Dunnett, an entirely different kind of teacher. Miss Dunnett had short, wavy brown hair; she wasn't tall and she wasn't short; she wasn't thin and she wasn't fat; she wasn't pretty and she wasn't unpleasant to look at. In short, she was thoroughly average in appearance. It was in her attitudes that she was remarkable.

The first morning she opened the class she brought out a vicious-looking yardstick, slapped it across her arm, and said, "I am the teacher and I will not tolerate anything in the way of misconduct in this school."

There had never been any misconduct in the school. The students knew what was expected of them and generally carried out whatever studies were demanded of them.

Miss Dunnett continued: "My brother said, when I took over this school, that I should bring both a rod and a ruler."

The children stared at her slack-jawed. "What on earth is she talking about?" they wondered. This concept of a teacher was so foreign, she might as well have been an alien from another planetary system. They were country children who had been taught by parents and neighbours and the charming Miss Devlin. None of those adults had ever carried a rod or a ruler; they simply taught the children what the children wanted to know and the kids got on with the job of learning.

Miss Dunnett effectively alienated her students and shut them down within ten minutes of arriving at her new school. Happily, her tenure was short-lived. Her pugnacious attitude was matched only by her inability to teach. When the district inspector arrived on a regular visit he was appalled at the poor progress the students had made in the two months she'd been in charge. Miss Dunnett was summarily dismissed and replaced by Miss Case.

Miss Case ran a good class until the school closed a year later at the end of Merve's third school year. The two oldest students graduated and a family with three children moved away. That left only six students—not enough to keep the school going.

The next closest school, North Cedar, was an additional three miles north and too far for a young child to walk twice a day, so Christina enrolled Merve in the British Columbia correspondence course. Merve completed his education right through high school studying in the familiar surroundings of his own living room. In many ways, the correspondence course gave Christina's son the best education she could possibly have wished for.

You either had to wait a week for the mail to bring you the answer to a question or you got out and researched it yourself and found the answer. The head teacher of the correspondence course, Mr. Hargreaves, very quickly realized that because my parents had lots of books available—and knew where to get books—that I was a prime candidate for coaching on how to find my own information. He always encouraged me to get out there and find the answer, even if it was an answer different from what he had. He acknowledged that different people had different answers for different things. That was acceptable if I quoted the source; then he knew I'd researched it.

Hargreaves was an inspiration and a wonderful teacher. Merve never met him, even though he continued to correspond with him long after he graduated.

Merve's life during those years wasn't all work and study. He experienced all the various aches, pains, and mishaps of the growing-up process in the usual ways. Some were fun.

Maggie and her brother Duncan and I had a contest one time to see who could squirt the farthest. We stood back to back to back on a big tree stump. I don't know what brought it up and one of us said something about boys being able to squirt and Maggie said, "Well, girls can too."

Well, we didn't believe it so we stood in this circle and squirted. Then we got down with a stick and measured and by golly if she didn't have us beaten – by about three inches! That took some of the braggadocio out of us.

Some were terrifying.

At that time most parents were horribly reticent to talk about sex. So Mom and Dad got a book: What a Young Boy Should Know, *written by Judge Ben B. Lindsay, a Supreme Court judge of the United States—of all the crazy people to write about sex. And he wrote a book that scared the living daylights out of me. Crazier still, he also wrote* What a Young Girl Should Know. *Well, I never read it but I know it scared the girls as badly as the boy book scared me.*

According to Judge Ben B. Lindsay, if you had a wet dream, you were doomed. Of course, Merve had never had a wet dream until he read Judge Lindsay's book. Then he had one and it terrified him. He knew he had to stop doing it; it was a terrible sin and he was about to go to hell—but how to stop?

There was only one solution. If he didn't sleep, he wouldn't dream and couldn't have wet dreams. So instead of going to bed, Merve would close his bedroom door at night, slip out the window, and go down to the lake. There he'd get into the rowboat and ply the oars up and down the lake most of the night.

One day Merve was out hunting with one of his adult friends, Bill Whitta. Bill had never married and had no children of his own. But he was a fatherly kind of man and easy to talk to because he never talked down to children.

Merve brought up the whole sex business. Whitta smiled. "All of us have had that experience. The reason is that you are growing up and sexual relations would be possible. But you're too young to be involved in them and not mature enough to take care of the consequences. You shouldn't be producing children yet—you're too young. You don't have the knowledge or the income. But nature's telling you you're capable of producing a family, so let nature do her thing. If you have a wet dream, so what. Get a towel and mop it up."

Judge Ben B. Lindsay's book, *What Every Young Boy Should Know*, was the first of two books Merve Wilkinson ever burned. The other burning came years later.

☆ ☆ ☆

Merve was ready to graduate from Grade Twelve in 1929, a few months before his sixteenth birthday. Along with about a dozen other correspondence students, he was given notice to turn up to write his final exam at the Quennell high school.

A small group of strangers congregated in the room just before the appointed hour of 9:00 a.m. It was a lovely late June day. The teacher who was there to supervise the young people was a man by the name of Oswald Wardle.

I found out afterwards, as I got to know more people in Nanaimo, that he was one of the outstanding teachers in the city. And I could see why. We were all in there and none of us knew each other. So you're plunked down to write a very important exam in completely unfamiliar surroundings, in front of a teacher you've never met before, and you had no idea what he was like—all in all, it was a frightening situation.

Oswald Wardle was aware of his charges' trepidation. He began class by reading an amusing story he'd just come across. Within ten minutes, the entire classroom was rocking with laughter. The tension evaporated. Students who'd been complete strangers ten minutes earlier glanced at each other furtively through their giggles and recognized a kindred soul.

When Wardle finished reading, he asked for comments from the class. The students bandied a few jokes back and forth and by 9:30, Wardle deemed the group ready to begin.

"Well, folks, it's time to get down to business," he said. "I've got an exam paper for each one of you. Please feel perfectly relaxed. I'm not your teacher, I'm just supervising this operation. I have some homework to do from my regular class and I'm going to be working right here at my desk while you work away at yours. I hope you all have success. I'm quite sure you will."

With that, Oswald Wardle handed out the papers. None of the students had a bit of difficulty doing their best work. At the end of the test, as the students handed in their papers, Wardle said, "Well this looks great. I hope to see you all somewhere along the way again and thanks for being in my class this morning."

Merve did well. His average mark of 85 percent would have been even higher if he hadn't done so poorly in Latin, only sneaking in a passing grade by a point or two. It wasn't until years later that he became intensely interested in Latin—not so much the language as the study of ancient Roman history. Mathematics, physics, science, and literature were his strengths.

And I really didn't have to strain to get those marks, so it spoke very well for the correspondence course. There have to be some success stories along the way and those two, the correspondence course with its emphasis on self-reliance and the teacher who—by the grace of God—sat there while we wrote our exams, added up to a real success story for everyone in that room.

Merve Wilkinson graduated from high school and bumped headfirst into the Great Depression. William Wilkinson was temporarily out of work as were so many others in the country. A university education was out of the question, so Merve entered a market that was swamped with men looking for jobs.

Christina and William had always encouraged their son to work hard and to take advantage of opportunities that came his way. What came his way most often was farm work from the surrounding neighbours. Someone always needed an extra pair of hands and Merve's were willing.

Merve rebuilt fences, drove horses, picked fruit, and harvested potatoes. He earned about $50 to $60 a month, which was very good money for those days. He did well because he was self-reliant. No one had to watch over him to make sure the job got done right. When a farmer gave him a task, Merve figured out a way to do it. He enjoyed doing a good job and he liked to please.

The farmer could turn over his herd of cows to Merve while he was away for a week and know that they'd be milked and that Merve would put the milk through the separator and sterilize the equipment. When the farmer came back he'd say "Thank you" and offer a ten dollar bill—or five dollars if that was all he could afford—but he'd make up for it in other ways. Maybe he had a bit of fishing tackle he wasn't using, or he'd pass along some shotgun shells because he knew Merve liked to hunt.

Merve enjoyed the odd jobs, but he dearly wanted to find some field that would lead him to a career. Serendipity brought along a job with the telephone company. It wasn't a career path, but it provided an opportunity to broaden his scope.

While Merve was still taking his high-school correspondence course, the locals had attempted to get telephone lines brought to their homes, but the phone company only had enough money to put in a mile of poles to serve a twelve-mile line.

So the company came up with an idea that it presented to the local people. It would put in the mile of line. Then it would supply the residents with the material to put in the rest of the line at wholesale prices. The company would give the locals the assistance and advice they'd need to install the lines themselves. Then the phone company would come in and hook up the line without charging a hook-up fee or billing for the new service.

The residents agreed that all of them would put in their share of hours in putting up the line and would do their own maintenance. Of course some folks were physically incapable of doing that, so their share of the work was divided amongst the others.

Until they got the hang of it, maintenance was a major problem. Whenever the wind blew up, the line broke. The locals figured out that you couldn't stretch the wire as tight when you strung it on trees as when you installed it on poles, so they spliced an extra piece of wire in and let the line sag.

There were three people on the line who couldn't do their own maintenance: the elderly Wilson couple, Minard Hill who owned the Yellow Point Lodge and was too busy to do the work himself, and Mrs. Sunnus, a widow with young children. They arrived at an agreement that they would pay Merve to keep up the telephone lines for them.

Merve learned how to balance a sixteen-foot ladder on a bicycle hurtling over gravel roads. He checked the lines after every storm. The widow gave Merve what she could afford, which wasn't very much; the Wilsons could afford a bit more; and Minard Hill, who had quite a bit of line, paid him handsomely by the hour. Merve earned decent money while he gained all sorts of practical experience with telephone wires.

During the Christmas and New Year season of 1930 that experience would prove very useful. That year Vancouver Island was hit by a week of tremendous rains followed by a windstorm gusting up to 90 miles per hour. No sooner had the wind really picked up than it started to snow; about sixteen inches fell in less than 24 hours. Every telephone line on Vancouver Island was out. Nothing could get through, not even an emergency call. Merve woke up on the morning after the snowfall and assessed the situation.

"You know what," he said to his father. "I think I'll hike into town to the telephone office and see if they need any ground crew."

"Well, it's a long hike, but go for it," William said. "They just might need you in a big way."

Christina packed him a lunch and a hot thermos, and Merve set off to walk the ten miles through knee-deep snow. It was still dark when he set out and he got there at about 10:45 a.m.

Merve had been to the office many times to pick up material to repair the lines, so Leo Griggs, the manager, knew him well.

"Boy are we ever glad to see you," Griggs said. "We have two crews coming from Vancouver on the noon boat and we need two ground men. We have one lad lined up and you'll be our second. Sign here."

Griggs said he'd take Merve on for as long as they needed him, but first he'd need better clothing than what he was wearing. And there was certainly no time to hike back home.

"Go over to Harvey Murphy's store—you know them—and get an outfit. Tell them to bill it to us. We'll take it off your first four paycheques so it doesn't hit you too hard. We know you'll be on at least that long."

Merve got what he needed and grabbed an extra bite of lunch at the cafeteria counter before going back to the telephone company office. Twenty minutes later the crews arrived from Vancouver. The crew foremen, Harvey Sodder and Walter Manson, flipped a coin for their ground men. Sodder won Merve. Not that it mattered much; the two crews worked together most of the time anyway.

They spent the first three days sawing out trees alongside the highway crews and stringing duplex cord between the broken lines. The work was daunting. Like most companies that were short of cash during the Depression, the telephone company had delayed replacing old poles that had seen better days. Only one in five poles was capable of standing up to any kind of wind. Hundreds of poles were lying flat on the ground with wires tangled into a mass of snarls.

For four days Merve and Tom, the other ground man, sat in the back of the truck, paying out duplex cord and hollering to the driver every now and then, "Hey, hold it! We've got to put in a splice!" And they'd go on to a new spool. They put in 90,000 feet of wire in four days and got two circuits working: one to Port Alberni and one to Duncan.

We met the Port Alberni boys laying duplex in Coombs, so we pulled back there and headed south. The line to Port Alberni went in first because Alberni had the big mills and those were very important lines. We wound south for two days and by that time Victoria had reached Duncan.

They laid two circuits to Duncan and then put in a third emergency circuit. But none of the lines were residential. In a sense, those first lines were all emergency circuits for use by hospitals, police, and firehalls. It took months to get private lines up and running again.

Merve worked for the telephone company for seven months. It was a fine job for a young man. Merve thought the crews and bosses were great guys all around. One Irish chap by the name of Bill Denim showed up for work every day wearing a bow tie, a nice clean shirt, and spotless trousers. He explained his unusual get-up by saying, "At this stage in my life I've earned the right to wear this sort of thing. The manager can wear them and he's not half as important to the telephone system as I am. If he had to string a wire, there'd be no service. I can make a telephone work and he can't."

Chapter 4

Powell River Days

The telephone company had to let Merve go after repairs were completed, and he went right back to doing odds and ends for his neighbours. Then in 1933 the provincial elections were held and the Co-operative Commonwealth Federation (CCF) won seven seats in the legislature and almost a third of the popular vote, becoming the official opposition. The CCF was a force in the province for many years, even after 1961 when the party reorganized itself as the New Democratic Party. Merve considered the CCF an excellent party that attracted all the bright young left-leaning people, including him.

Powell River was in one of the ridings that had elected a CCF member to the legislature. The owners of the Powell River Company, a giant pulp mill, were not pleased with the results. The fact was, as Merve was soon to find out, the Powell River Pulp and Paper Company had reason to fear a co-operative federation of workers.

Merve heard about the Powell River Company from Leo Griggs, his former boss at the telephone company. "They are taking on some people up in Powell River," he said. "There's quite a turnover in labour there and I'm not sure just why. But I know they are employing some people. If you're interested in going, my brother is head of the telephone company up there. He knows the paymaster. I could call him and tell him how satisfied we were with your work. That could help you."

Eager for work of any kind, Merve said he would take a chance on Powell River. He had no idea what he was getting into.

"I don't think it will do you any harm," William said when Merve talked it over with his parents. "But son, I'll tell you what to do. Go up there with a bit more than a limited amount of money. These hiring fellows are kind of funny at times, and I don't know what's happening up there. Just buy yourself a return ticket—it might come in handy."

48

Merve listened to his father, bought a return ticket, and took the boat to Powell River. Approaching from the water, the whole of Powell River was laid out for Merve's inspection. The pulp mill overshadowed everything. It consisted of an enormous collection of buildings spread out along the waterfront. They belched steam and stench hundreds of feet into the air. The smell was a mixture of rotting cabbages and decaying meat.

Merve's feelings were mixed. There was the excitement of knowing he could find work here, coupled with the horror of the sight. When he was finally able to tear his eyes away from the monster, Merve saw spotless white houses tiered up the hillside overlooking the water. The town's setting overlooking the Strait of Georgia and backed by towering forests and the coastal mountain range was pretty beyond belief.

As the boat drew closer to the dock Merve became aware of the sounds—an overwhelming cacophony of groans, screeches, crunches, and bangs. It was a noise he would learn to live with 24 hours a day.

His first order of business was to see the paymaster, a Mr. Flett, who did the hiring.

"Oh yes, Griggs phoned me about you," the paymaster said. "I understand you've been working for the phone company."

"Yes."

"For how long?"

"Seven months."

"Obviously they were quite happy with your work."

"Well, I try to do a good job and apparently I did."

"Well, I don't have anything today, but drop around tomorrow morning between eight and nine. We do have times when we're a man short and then we put somebody on to fill that role for the day. You can work your way into the company that way."

"Well, that's fine. That sounds okay," Merve said.

"That way, too, if you ever do get on steady, you'll have worked in several departments and will have a good idea of what the whole process is about. So this has a bit of an advantage."

Merve dutifully arrived back the following morning.

"We need a man on the dock this afternoon. You'll be wheeling paper."

"Fine, I'll be there," Merve said.

Merve wheeled paper for the afternoon shift. He went back to the paymaster's office the next morning and the next and the next.

There was no more work and Merve had the rest of each day free to meet people in town. Powell River was packed with men—almost 300 of them—all lined up for jobs at the mill. Merve got to talking with these fellows.

"How long have you been trying to get on?" he asked them.

"I've been here six months."

"How much work do you get?"

"Just enough to keep me."

"Uh-huh." Merve pondered that and approached another man. "How long have you been around town here?"

"Oh … about a year."

"How much work have you had in that year?"

"A couple of days a month. I'm just getting by."

Merve's curiosity was piqued. He talked to about ten men, all with the same story. It didn't take him long to fit the pieces together. The mill management was using this big pool of available labour as a threat. The worst thing a worker could expect to find when he arrived for his shift was an empty slot where his punch card had been. It was the only notice he'd ever get that he was fired.

When I put the picture together it showed a real piece of exploitation. The labour situation allowed them to get away with it. There was no union of course.

So I went in on the fifth day and I said, "Mr. Flett, I see what's happening in this town. If there is an opportunity here, I will stay. If not, I have a return ticket in my wallet."

Flett looked at Merve long and hard. "Come back at two o'clock this afternoon," he said.

When Merve came back, Flett said, "We have an opening in the grinding room. Be there tomorrow morning at 7:30. In the meantime, go up to the hospital and have a medical."

Merve was in, thanks to a return ticket and the uncanny self-assurance he'd been born with.

He was assigned to Frank Oldale's shift in the grinding room, where logs were lifted out of the water and ground down to pulp. "How did you get on so quick?" Oldale wanted to know.

"I was not going to stay here and be a sucker. I was going to move on. I guess the record of performance I came with from the previous company meant they didn't want to pass up on me. That's why I'm here."

For Merve, the grinding room at the Powell River Company was an altogether different classroom. It was here that his education in human nature was rounded out. On his first day he met the superintendent: "So-glad-to-meet-you-if-you-work-hard-you'll-go-far," was his patter. Implicit in this attitude was the warning: Don't question anybody or what they're doing. Just do what you're told and you'll go places.

Merve wasn't twenty yet, but he was a skeptic when it came to anything or anyone promising a good life that required no thought. He quickly figured out the system. The men who rated the highest were least likely to go places.

Merve's job was to take wood out of the flume and pile it up for the grinders. He worked up and down the flume and got to know all the grinders. Ollie Svenson was one of the best grinders in the place.

"Ollie, how long have you worked here?" Merve asked.

"I've been a grinder for twelve years."

"No change? No chance for a step up?"

"Oh no, I'm too good. They need me here."

Merve asked Tony, "How long have you been on this?"

"I've been here fourteen years."

And I said to myself, "Uh-huh, Wilkinson, you're not going to be here grinding wood for fourteen years." I made up my mind pretty quick on that one. When I did get a grinder job, I ground good pulp but I learned very quickly not to let the grinder run me. I ran the grinder.

The mill's way of working the grinders was to load the machine's pockets to the brim and run them full tilt all day. At the end of the shift, the man running the machine went home in a state of collapse. Merve's way was to slow the machines down to a reasonable speed so that he could put in a decent day's work without stretching himself to a point of inhuman stress.

Interestingly, the faster the grinders worked the more pulp they wasted. Merve's method extracted more pulp and a better grade of pulp. But the company didn't care about waste. Wood was cheap and plentiful. Every 24 hours, 24 tons of pulp spilled into Strait of Georgia as waste.

The superintendent didn't much care about anything other than having the men working at breakneck speed. He also had the rather nasty habit of calling around at a new man's home while he was working and telling the wife that her man would be out of a job unless she was very nice to him.

His nickname was "Papa." When Merve first heard it, he couldn't figure it out. "Why do you call him 'Papa'?" he asked one of the men. "He's one of the most unlovable men I've ever met."

"You've got the wrong end of the handle," the man said. "We call him Papa because he's got so many illegitimate children in town."

"Thanks for the tip," Merve said. And he meant it. His thoughts had begun to turn very seriously to marriage.

But "Papa" was only one factor that made working conditions unbearable. There was no ventilation in the grinding room. It was full of steam, which wouldn't have been so bad if not for the shipworms. The wood that came into the grinding room was full of the worms, most of them dead. When they were subjected to intense heat and steam, the flesh cooked, filling the air with the all-pervasive odour of rotten meat.

Merve worked in the room for two years. He didn't put out the quantity of pulp the other grinders did, and Frank Oldale, the shift foreman, was aware of it. He looked at the test results almost daily and saw that the pulp Merve turned out was uniform and even, but his quantities weren't up to scratch. When a pulp tester left the company, Oldale said, "Merve, how would you like to go into pulp testing?"

"Really?" Merve asked.

"Yes, you're very meticulous. I'm sure you'd make a good one and you'd do well in there."

"That sounds great," Merve said. "I'm all for it."

Just as he had so carefully planned, Merve moved on because unlike the "best" grinders, he was eminently replaceable. In his new job he had to make sure the pulp fibres that came out of the grinders weren't too short or too long. Depending on the grade of fibres, machines were speeded up or slowed down to compensate.

The superintendent of the grinding room wanted the machines to run full blast because he believed that meant productivity. The papermakers wanted the machines to run slow because then they'd get a finer grade of paper. The tests were redundant most of the time because no one paid attention to them.

The upshot of almost every test result was that there was too much coarse fibre being made and too much waste spilling into the Strait of Georgia. Merve had almost resigned himself to the

Merve enjoyed music and theatre all his life. Here, standing on the
right, he portrays a seaman first class in *The Treasure Hunt*,
a 1935 musical production in Powell River.

helplessness of the situation when the hated superintendent had to
go to Vancouver for an operation. He was gone for three months.
Bill McGilvary, the man who took over for him, was a curious person
with an open mind. He quickly noticed there was something lacking
in the pulp-to-wood ratio.

"You know, there's too much wood going through here for the
amount of pulp we're getting," he said to the testers.

The senior pulp tester said, "Bill, when the tide is low tonight,
go down to the end of the water pipe and have a look at what's
coming out."

Bill went down and came back on the double. "Do you have an
empty 500 cc container?"

"Yes, sure thing."

"Can I have it, quick?"

He grabbed it and raced off. A minute later he was back in the
testing facility with the container full of water and wood fibre. "Will
you run me a test on this quick or do I have to take it to the lab
upstairs?"

"No, Bill, we can do it here."

Bill left. "Merve, we're holding on to a stick of dynamite here,"
the senior pulp tester said.

Merve knew it. "You know what we should do? We should take 250 ccs and run our tests on that. Save the other half and keep it in reserve."

"Good idea."

They ran the test and found 8.3 tons of waste in an eight-hour period.

"Good God, look at all the timber we're wasting," Bill said when he saw the results. "It's amazing!"

When the upstairs lab men got hold of the results, they didn't just think it was amazing; they plain didn't believe it. "Your tests are faulty," they said.

So Merve handed them the 250 ccs he'd kept on ice. "Test it for yourself," he suggested.

They did and came back shaking their heads. "As a matter of fact, your results were low. We show 8.6 tons of waste."

Bill McGilvary made sweeping changes. For a while the machines ran at a reasonable rate. But only for a while. When the superintendent recovered from his eye operation, he edged the machines back up a bit at time until he had them running full tilt again and spewing waste into the harbour.

Chapter 5

Marriage and the Shaping of Ideals

It was in 1934 while he was working at the Powell River paper mill that Merve started thinking seriously of getting married. The girl he was considering was Catherine Mary Carpenter. She was tall and slim with thick, dark, curly hair. Her face was well chiselled. She had eyes that could dance with amusement or flash in anger. She had dignity tempered with humour—it was her humour that captured Merve's attention.

He had met Mary Carpenter at the Devinso Club, a youth group of the First United Church that he'd joined when he was about sixteen.

> We had a wonderful crowd of teenagers, late teens and early 20s. We went out on picnics and dance parties and so on. At that time, you didn't pair off into couples; you dated all the girls. Over the course of a few years, you'd taken them all out. So you gradually got to know a wide range of individuals and a wide range of personalities and you began to realize that out of this group of fifteen or twenty girls, there were ones you enjoyed being with more than the others. You felt more at ease ... more comfortable. You found you were interested in the same kind of music and the same kind of books.
>
> There were an awful lot of couples that came out of that club— ten or a dozen, I'd say—who lived with each other until they died. They were so well matched before they got married that they were perfect companions.

After three years of dating the various girls in the group, Merve had pretty well narrowed his field to Mary. Was he in love with Mary or was he just being sensible? Probably both. Merve wasn't the sort of man to be swept off his feet with emotion; he never had been before. There was logic and reasoning in everything he did. He may have loved Mary but he also weighed the situation carefully.

Her father, Captain Joe Carpenter, was a former military man with the militia. Back when Merve's mother was fighting off bullies at the picket lines, it was Captain Carpenter's detachment from Victoria that was called in to keep the peace.

Mary Carpenter and Merve Wilkinson had been raised with many of the same principles. They grew up with a solid work ethic and a good grounding in moral values. By the time Merve went to Powell River, he and Mary had become very good friends. There were no commitments, but they had an unspoken agreement. When Merve came home from time to time, he didn't wait long before calling Mary up and taking her out to a dance or a show. They exchanged letters at least once a week—not love letters—just the chat of everyday happenings.

They were in the process of falling in love.

But those things didn't happen as fast as they do today. The whole world was not speeded up. It took you longer. You started by liking the other person. You felt close to them, you put your arm around them, you hugged and you kissed them but you didn't go exploring. Most people kissed their girlfriend good-night and they didn't think anything too seriously of it. People didn't jump into bed with other people at the drop of a hat either. The possibility didn't even exist.

There was a difference in the style of life, in the amount of exercise we had at that time and also the diet. The thought never crossed our minds—not in the gang I grew up with, and I think we were a pretty representative gang. We were the sons and daughters of merchants and tradesmen: a cross section of the population. We all had chores at home and we all had things we did with our parents ... and we enjoyed doing them.

So Dad's painting the house and you'd do the big areas and not the trim. Well, you'd get quite a bit of paint on yourself, but after a little while you got around to the point where you were really proud of what you'd done.

You don't have that going on today. Kids today—their minds have become one-track. Back then, it was only if someone had a disease like diabetes that they'd be overweight. You didn't see the obesity you see today. Kids, even though they had less food, had good food. They had a healthy balanced diet. There were more places they could go. The beaches were open to everyone so instead of going off the rails, you'd all go down to the beach and swim.

One time we were up on the Forbidden Plateau—there were five of us boys and five girls who knew each other well. We were on a hike and it was a really warm day. We came out on a little ridge top and there was a shallow lake on both sides of it so we knew the water would be great. Well, we didn't have swimsuits—nobody told us you could swim on Forbidden Plateau. Anyway, these lakes looked so inviting that one of the girls said, "Hey, wouldn't it be fun to go skinny-dipping? Here, we'll stay on this side of the ridge and have a dip here, and you guys go down to the lake on the other side. We'll give you about ten minutes because the water will be cold."

So we took our watches off and we got to horsing around and having fun in the water and didn't realize that ten minutes was long up. First thing we know is there's a row of girls sitting on top of the hill saying, "Now we've got you guys. You don't dare come out. How are you going to get your clothes on?"

They sat there for a while and then said, "Well, we're not going to keep you much longer. The water must be getting pretty cold. We'll go back and give you ten minutes, but if you're not dressed in ten minutes, don't blame us for the consequences."

For Merve and his gang it was a simpler and more naïve life with no television and no computers with instant access to the Internet. But they were happy and healthy, and when they got married, their marriages tended to last a lifetime. It was almost a foregone conclusion that Mary and Merve would get married. But while Merve was in Powell River and Mary in Nanaimo, they dated other people too. Neither wanted to limit the other's social life, and Merve didn't want to pop the question until he felt steady and secure in his job.

He'd been at the Powell River Company a year when he and Mary started having serious conversations. Long-distance telephone calls had begun to supplement the weekly letters. Mary was a schoolteacher and was having difficulties with the principal at her school. She didn't like the way he ran the school and was ready to give up. "I can't get the principal's co-operation in any way," she told Merve. "And then when his system doesn't work, he jumps all over me."

When Merve went home for the Christmas holidays in 1933, one of the first things he did was visit Mary. He took her out to a show and then they went back to her house. Mary's mother and father excused themselves after a while. "Don't leave, Merve," the Captain said. "We've had a heavy day and we're going to bed. But stay if you like."

So Merve and Mary settled down side by side on the couch in front of the fire. "How are you feeling about this school situation now?" he asked.

"Not good," Mary admitted. "I think I'll try for a new school next year."

"Well, instead of doing that, instead of each of us going it alone, how about we do it together? Let's get married."

Mary didn't have to think about it. Her smile went from ear to ear. "Oh that's wonderful. Oh yes!"

Merve recalls the kiss that followed as being particularly good—and the one after that and the one after that one.

Merve went back to Powell River after the holidays hovering several inches above the ground. Although he didn't try it, he felt like he could have walked right across the Strait of Georgia. But his practical streak didn't let his heart get carried away. They had set the wedding date for the summer so that Mary could finish out her school year and Merve could find a place for them to live. Mary had few demands, but she did insist on electric lights and running water. In the Powell River of the 1930s it was entirely possible to have to put up with no water and no electricity and still pay a fair bit for rent.

Merve found an old employee's shack that belonged to a shingle mill on the outskirts of town. It was primitive, but it was alongside the dam and had a pretty view of the water. The most recent inhabitants had been transient loggers, and Merve had his work cut out for him to turn the shack into a home. The landlord agreed to take the cost of materials off the rent bill, and Merve painted the place, papered the walls, and cleaned it up well enough to make it habitable.

When Mary came to look it over she said, "This is fine. I can be quite happy here." And that was that.

The wedding took place in late July. Merve had arranged for two weeks off so that he and Mary could drive down the coast to San Francisco and back. The ceremony took place in St. Paul's church in Nanaimo. The church was packed. Merve was nervous, exhilarated, and overwhelmed by butterflies flying through his chest and stomach. There was a best man, a maid of honour, two pretty flower girls, and a church stuffed to the rafters with flowers.

She was so radiant, so happy ... she had a lovely white dress with a veil that trailed to the ground and a bouquet of flowers.

The reception was held at the Carpenter home in the garden that Mary's brothers had groomed to perfection just that morning.

Merve and Mary on their wedding day.

While they were trimming the lawn, Merve had been working on Mary's car. If it was going to get them to San Francisco and back, it would need new spark plugs and a water pump.

Merve and Mary spent their wedding night in a motel cabin in Mount Vernon. They had an old '26 Chevy and the open road ahead of them. What else could they have asked for?

Two weeks later, after an idyllic honeymoon, they set up house in Powell River.

Perhaps it was his break away from the mill, but Merve could now see that few of the workers had any faith in the pulp and paper industry. Some people, even some in management positions, had a great deal of integrity, but the industry itself had none. The company's policy was to use intimidation to keep the employees in line. There were no unions, so they could get away with pretty well anything they liked. Dissenters were put on blacklists that were circulated between industries. A dissenter was anyone who didn't like the way he'd been spoken to and spoke back, or a person who had expressed opinions that the management didn't like, or a person who was politically connected to anything less than the extreme right. You didn't have to be a communist to be labelled left wing, although there were quite a few good communists around.

Then there were the wages—not that they were the best to speak of—but the workers were expected to give all the money they made back to the company by buying from the company store. If they chose to shop elsewhere, they were marked men; they'd never get a promotion. Management wasn't secretive about that fact.

A story that made the rounds of all the mills was about an incident at the pulp mill in Ocean Falls. Crown Zellerbach owned the mill. Six months after hiring a new manager, Zellerbach made a trip to the mill to see how things were going. The new manager was out to impress.

"Mr. Zellerbach," he said, "we've got it rigged now so that we get 96 cents of every employee's dollar back."

Zellerbach snorted, "Why don't you get the other four?"

That story could be taken two ways, but most folks believed it was Zellerbach's way of keeping the manager in line, too. It underscored the stranglehold the mills had on their labour.

The working conditions were brutal at best. Some departments were good enough if there was a good man in charge. Most departments ran under the premise that the men were no better than animals. You put them to work and if they died, so what? If they got ground up into pulp, who cared? If they drowned in the flume, it didn't matter. Others could take their places.

When management of the Powell River Company shifted to the Bell-Irving family, conditions changed to a degree. The Bell-Irvings were a dynastic Vancouver family that had made their name in real estate. They felt that the mill was operating in an old-fashioned manner and the way to improve it was to bring in an efficiency expert. Merve had gone back to work as a grinder and was right there when the expert came into that department. Old Mr. K, the hated superintendent, escorted him into the room. The expert stepped through the door, took one whiff of the steam and stench, and said, "Good Lord! How do you expect anybody to work in conditions like this? First thing is get a ventilating fan ... And fix some of these windows so they open. Instead of having fellows fishing wood out of the water so they get wet, take the flume out and put in buggies—do it dry."

To K's objections he just said, "It'll pay for itself."

"How can it pay for itself if you're laying more money out?"

"You'll have workmen that will do a better job; then you'll get your money back."

Bill McGilvary, the assistant superintendent, was delighted with the suggestions. "This is wonderful," he said. "We should have been doing this ten years ago."

A month later, with windows open, ventilating fans in place, and buggies hauling in the wood, production went up 10 percent per man.

But to survive and keep your job at the mill, a man had to be a Dr. Jekyll and Mr. Hyde. Merve, like most of the others, pretended to go along with it. However, his resentment at having to be a two-faced individual was strong, and whenever he had the chance, he went as far as he dared in saying, "I don't like that and I don't agree with it."

Every department had a private detective hired to keep track of possible labour unrest. They were supposed to be deep undercover, but they all came from the same detective agency and usually wore the same sort of clothes. The men spotted them quickly and made a game of feeding them false information.

If someone were a real company man—a "suckhole" as he was called—the men would tell the detective about him, "Hey, you'd better watch that one. I think he's a communist."

★ ★ ★

There wasn't a time in Merve's life when he wasn't a sworn anti-militarist. By the time he was a young married man, he was clearly a free thinker, a man devoted to peace and a man who passionately supported justice and goodness. He could have stepped out of the pages of a Louisa May Alcott novel. But men like Merve Wilkinson weren't unusual in the 1930s, especially not in small towns and rural areas. They were men who believed in lending a helping hand to a neighbour. One of Merve's favourite sayings is: "If you help a man get to the top of the hill, you'll wind up there yourself."

In 1936, Merve's passion for justice, his abhorrence of war, and his sense of duty to his new wife clashed over the Spanish Civil War. And though Merve didn't go to Spain to fight in the war, it had a profound effect on him and further shaped his already deeply ingrained liberalism.

> *The war was a lesson in politics and a lesson in whom you could or could not trust. It was also a lesson in values, in principles—the whole bit.*

Spain had always been ruled from the top down, either by a monarchy or a military dictatorship. In the 1930s, however, it became a republic, and when a democratic election was called in 1936, there were an enormous number of parties, with half a dozen on the left and as many on the right and in the middle. The Spanish people were passionate about politics and turned out in large numbers on election day. To the best of anyone's knowledge, the vote was entirely fair and democratic. The left-wing parties received about 80 percent of the popular vote and formed an alliance.

The new government was a great success. It began to inspire the hopes of its citizens and of people around the world with its sincere attempts to liberalize old legislation while recognizing the value of all individuals instead of just those with money and power. Some pundits were beginning to hold the new Spanish government up as a model for the kind of government people all over the world were calling for.

But old orders don't die easily. Benito Mussolini and Adolf Hitler were both vying for the opportunity to be leaders in Europe. A new, liberal, democratic regime didn't fit in with their ideologies. Hitler, in particular, was solidly on the right. In fact, his policy of recognizing the needs of the wealthiest over the needs of the poorest was looked upon very favourably by a certain British conservative element. Hitler's policies favoured big business; the new Spanish government did not.

Hitler was the fair-haired boy in the United States, Britain, and a large part of France. He was considered a bulwark against communism, and nothing terrified big business more than Marxist ideals. Hitler and Mussolini were also eager to preview a war, so when General Francisco Franco and the extreme right decided they would not accept the Spanish election and started a revolution, they lent Franco their full support.

The revolution stirred up an international controversy. For the first time, the military was revolting to overthrow a democratically elected government—a government clearly supported by the people. This went completely against everything people knew about revolutions, which were normally fought by the oppressed to overthrow an autocratic rule.

The big world powers were quick to take sides. Canada went along with the United States, Britain, and the right-wing element in France in throwing their weight against the Spanish government. Canada made no official statements but put an embargo on many products that went to Spain and assisted in naval blockades.

In one case there was a Spanish ship that was stopped, searched by the U.S. Navy, and then sunk. That really antagonized people all over the world—the idea that a civilian ship on the high seas could be stopped and sunk because it was going to a Spanish port—its home port. That really was an atrocity that the world should have reacted more strongly against.

Merve wrestled with a multitude of philosophical questions: Do you stand for right or do you stand for wrong? Can you mix the two? Can you have a mixture that's acceptable or is it not possible? When he began to answer his own questions, he realized that for the first time in his life, he felt so strongly that he was ready to join his friends who had gone off to fight alongside the elected government in the Spanish Civil War.

I've never been a militarist. I've no use for them. I see them as nothing but tools of autocracy and greed all down through the ages. But I was really torn. I hated militarism, and yet here was a fight that obviously needed to be fought. It was a weighty decision.

If Mary had not been pregnant, Merve most certainly would have gone to Spain. His conscience told him his first obligation was to his family, but he was determined to find other ways to lend support.

Those of us who stayed, we found ways and means of donating money and collecting materials, particularly first-aid and medical supplies, and thanks to the wonderful co-operation of the leftist part of France, they managed to get most of it across the border ... I had a very minor part to play in the Spanish Civil War and yet it was an important part of my life. It generated a tremendous amount of anger and disgust in my feelings for people who will claim to be democrats and honest people and will then resort to this underhanded technique. They were undermining something they had no knowledge of and they weren't about to even try to get that knowledge. I felt that was one of the great injustices of all time. And if it had been handled differently, the Second World War with all its atrocities might not even have occurred.

Chapter 6

From Powell River to Brother Twelve

As the months went by at the Powell River Pulp and Paper Co. paper mill, Merve stepped closer and closer to the line in what he dared to do and say. He dared because he and Mary had an escape hatch. Just about the time he was getting set for his wedding day, Merve had bought 147 acres of forest including land—a portion of which would eventually become Wildwood.

In one way or another, how that land came to be purchased was tied up with the story of the infamous Brother Twelve. Brother Twelve's real name was Edward Arthur Wilson. In the 1920s he believed that the world was ready to collapse. His plan was to create a haven for some very special people, which he would call the Aquarian Foundation. He felt that Cedar, a small community just south of Nanaimo near Yellow Point, was far enough from the major centres to be safe. It had a good climate and soil that would grow most anything.

The Aquarian Foundation was one of many doomsday groups formed at that time. There was a saying in the United States: "Roosevelt or Revolution!" Some wealthy people believed a revolution was so imminent they kept an airplane fuelled and ready to take off at a moment's notice. People flocked to the Aquarian Foundation. It attracted those who believed society as they knew it was ending. Among them were skilled weavers, artists, and people who could teach art; there were writers who could keep the language alive, and an amazing assortment of talented and intelligent people.

Brother Twelve offered these people a place to live where they could build a home on a piece of common property. They could have their own gardens and live their own lives. But some things were pooled—things like skills and money.

Brother Twelve set up the Foundation in the mid 1920s. He and his followers were well thought of in the community and functioned

Three of the governors of the Aquarian Foundation at their first
general meeting, July 25, 1927. Left to right: Joseph Benner,
publisher of *The Sun*, Akron Ohio; Maurice Von Platen,
who sold Merve his land; and Edward Wilson (Brother Twelve).

as a colony for seven years before it began to fall apart. The demise
began when Brother Twelve claimed he was the reincarnation of an
Egyptian god who was going to mate with a woman and produce a
replica of Isis. He had a lot of cash by then, mostly in gold.

*I can remember being so mad at him at one time. I was about fourteen.
The old farmer's co-op was going very well at that time. The Aquarian
Foundation had a lot of agriculturally minded people. They needed
a lot of hoes, rakes, harrows, tractors—things the co-op could get for
them. So they joined the co-op. And they joined it on the basis of the
accounts being paid every 30 days. Brother Twelve always paid in
gold.*

*He arrived at our house one time when Mom and Dad had a
picnic arranged. We were going with another family and two of my
friends, Dave and Rebecca. They were fun to be with and I was
really looking forward to it.*

Well, I'll be darned if Brother Twelve didn't arrive Saturday night to pay his account at the co-op. Instead of going to the office Monday morning, he came down to Dad's place on Saturday night with $3,000 in gold pieces. And I was so mad at Brother Twelve over that because there was no chance of going on the picnic with all this stashed away in the house. I was livid with the old guy!

Shortly after that, Brother Twelve dropped in for a musical evening while Merve was studying for an exam. Brother Twelve stopped by Merve's desk and looked over some of his papers.

"I hope you don't mind my looking at these?" he asked.

"Oh no, Mr. Wilson, go ahead. What do you think of them?"

"You're doing well," he said. "But one thing, Merve. You can never learn enough. You can go on learning all your life, but you'll never know it all. So keep it up. Don't ever stop."

That piece of advice stuck with Merve for a lifetime. It came just after Brother Twelve claimed to have visited the planet Aquarius. The story is explained as mad rambling by most who have heard it. But there are those who wonder.

Brother Twelve disappeared for three days. Until then he'd simply been known as Mr. Wilson. When he came back, he told about being picked up in a flying saucer and flown to a planet called Aquarius. They travelled for 36 hours at seven or eight times the speed of light using the power of the ether. He spent a day on the planet. He described a very beautiful place similar to Earth but with a milder climate. When his guides saw how interested he was, they offered to take him to the eleven brothers who ruled the planet. They took him into a large building. The Brothers questioned where he was from and who he was. He told them about the Aquarian Foundation.

"What is that?" they asked. "This planet is named Aquarius. When did you decide on the name for your foundation?"

"Why, four or five years ago."

"Tell us more about it. What does your society aim to do?"

Wilson gave them the syllabus. The Brothers passed it around, nodding their approval. "This is wonderful," they said. "How are you doing with it?"

"Very well. We are 400 strong and growing. And every year I go on a world tour and I always come back with 20 or 30 more members."

"It sounds like you're doing very creditable work," the Brothers said. "We would like to honour you. We will name you Brother Twelve, and if you return to Aquarius again—which we hope will be possible—you will sit with us in our government."

Brother Twelve was a smart enough man to have lost himself in the woods for three days. On the other hand, there were very reliable people nearby who said that they smelled a funny, hot odour at the time he departed. That smell has been recorded in other sightings of flying saucers. What really happened?

All Merve can say is that his own memories of Brother Twelve are fond ones. Years later when he came across a book about Brother Twelve written by a man who claimed to be his brother, Merve performed the second book-burning ceremony of his life. Just for starters, Brother Twelve was an only child. The book suffered the same fate as Judge Ben B. Lindsay's *What Every Boy Should Know*.

Merve's future forest was owned by Maurice Von Platen, one of the men who belonged to—and later helped break up—the Aquarian Foundation. Von Platen, a native New Yorker, had a hole in his heart: an inoperable condition at that time. As a boy, he had worked as a printer's devil, or helper. He was an ingenious fellow and it didn't take him long to realize he could speed up the printing process considerably by altering the way the machine worked. He patented his invention, which became known as the Von Platen Press. It was in use for many years and made him a tidy fortune. Being a bit of a socialist, Von Platen refused to sell his patent to Hearst or Thompson or any of the other publishing giants. He'd put a price of something like 1/100 or 1/1000 percent on every word printed on his press as his royalty. In Von Platen's opinion, royalties were far better than having a chunk of money all at once. At the same time, anyone with a small press could afford a Von Platen press. It didn't sound like a lot at the time he made the royalty agreement, but his invention sped up the presses to such a degree that millions and billions more words were printed. Von Platen became a millionaire several times over. His patent lasted until he and his wife were both dead. After that, the royalties were bequeathed to a children's charity.

Von Platen was a tinkerer. He couldn't do heavy work so he repaired pipe organs and he was good at it. He travelled all over the world fixing pipe organs. Along the way he came across Brother Twelve and the Aquarian Foundation. He approved of their principles, but when he saw those principles being perverted, he helped pull the Foundation apart.

Von Platen loved to fish, but he couldn't row a boat, so when Merve wasn't studying, he rowed him around the lake. Von Platen formed a close bond with Merve and with Merve's parents. It was a happy way of life for Von Platen for years. He had people living on his land for a short while. They'd framed a house and put a roof on it so there was emergency shelter if it was needed. He put his millions to good use, spending his money almost as quickly as it came in. He contributed to a long list of charities. When his neighbours needed help, the help arrived as though by a miracle. Once a neighbouring farmer's horse died right in the middle of planting. The next day a horse trader arrived with a horse the right size and beautifully trained.

"This is your horse," the trader said.

"I don't have the money for the horse," the farmer said.

"You don't need the money for the horse. It's already paid for."

It took that farmer five years to find out that it was Von Platen who had paid for it. For a millionaire, $350 for a horse was nothing. For a farmer, it was the world.

One time there was a $50,000 donation made to the Nanaimo hospital. No one could trace it, but it was suspected to be a Von Platen contribution.

Von Platen could afford the best medical care in North America, and the day inevitably came when the doctors examined him and told him to give up travelling and go home to New York. A medical procedure was being developed that could help him. In the meantime, he was to rest. He decided to sell his land. He knew Merve loved the forest and that piece of land in particular. So in October 1933 he phoned William Wilkinson.

"Look, I'm going to be putting the property up for sale. No hurry, but if Merve wants it, he gets first option."

William told his son.

"Phone Mr. Von Platen right back," Merve said. "Tell him I would love to have it."

The going price at that time was $15 an acre. Von Platen was asking $1,500 for the 147 acres. Between them, Merve and Mary had saved $1,000, so they put the entire amount down on the land. Merve's mother put up the rest of the money and became a joint owner with Merve. Christina liked the idea of being a landowner

The old orchard slopes gently down to the shores of Quennell Lake. The Wildwood orchard was part of the original acreage Merve and Mary settled on.

and turned out to be a shrewd businesswoman. Although she only put up one-third of the money, she reasoned that she should have almost half the land—70 acres—because Merve and Mary owned the section that had shelter and a small orchard. Her land was undeveloped so therefore she should own more of it. Later, when Merve began working the forest, he paid Christina a small stumpage fee for the trees on her part of the property.

And that was why Merve Wilkinson, working in the mill under nearly unbearable conditions, began to speak up more and more. He joined the "Flying Squad," an underground group that was organizing the men into a force to be reckoned with. A small but not insignificant revolution was fomenting at the mill. The Flying Squad was organized by a man called Hodge, an electrical engineer from the Lower Mainland, who was also a member of the Communist Party. He taught the men well. The Flying Squad looked for rabble-rousers. If they found out that a man was in favour of the union and if he was willing to stick his neck out a bit, they'd instruct him to contact two more people. It all went in threes; it was safer that way. No more than three ever knew who you were or what you were up to.

The government in Victoria had just passed new labour laws. A company had to have a quorum of 60 percent of the work force to form a union. The conspiracy of three worked well. The Flying Squad sat down one night, toted up figures, and decided to take the chance. They contacted the authorities in Victoria who set up the vote. When they counted the ballots, 84 percent were in favour of unionizing the mill.

Merve left the mill before that final vote. Mary was pregnant, and Merve had been pegged as an agitator. It was Bill McGilvary who tipped Merve off.

"Merve," he said, "you've been talking pretty freely lately."

"Yes, I have, Bill, and I'll tell you and I'll tell Frank ... you've both been really nice guys. I'm planning to leave. I've got a piece of property of my own. I'm going to step out of the pulp industry and take up something else."

"Good for you. Go for it," Bill said. "I wish you luck. But don't be surprised if they can you."

Merve told his foreman, Frank Oldale, the next day and gave three weeks notice—a move that was unheard-of then. A foreman normally found out one of his men had quit when he simply didn't show up for work.

Merve handed in his notice to the foreman and the assistant superintendent but not to the superintendent, Mr. K. The grapevine being what it was, the superintendent soon learned of it.

Days before Merve was about to step out of the mill forever, Mr. K. stepped in front of him. "Well, Merve," he said, "you'll be going up to the new mill."

The "new" mill had a notorious reputation. The machines were geared to run twice the speed as the ones at the old mill.

"No, Mr. K. I won't be going up to the new mill," Merve said.

"What? Who the hell do you think runs this place?"

"You run it. But I won't be here, Mr. K., and I won't be going up to your new mill."

Mr. K. stomped off and that was the last Merve saw of him or the mill.

Chapter 7

A Commitment to Sustainable Forestry

By the time they left Powell River, Merve and Mary had accumulated a surprising array of possessions. When their friends and neighbours heard that the young couple was moving to a sizeable piece of land in the country, they donated all sorts of things they thought Merve and Mary might need.

The only economical way to get all their household possessions from Powell River to Nanaimo was by barge. Tugboat companies had routes all up and down the coast and charged by weight. However, there was no scale at Powell River, so the shipper and the wharfinger together estimated the weight and came to an agreement.

Merve got all his goods and chattels to the wharf a week before the barge came in. He knew that he could leave it there safely while he and Mary went ahead to set up house. He and the wharfinger had estimated $45 to ship the lot, so that's what Merve paid. But after Merve had left, his friend the mill blacksmith had a present delivered to the dock. It was a box of gear he'd made that included everything from gate hinges to chisels and hammers. The box weighed at least 500 pounds. Soon more boxes from other friends arrived, and by the time all was said and done, Merve figured he had inadvertently cheated the wharfinger out of freight charges for 1,000 pounds worth of goods.

On arrival at Yellow Point they stored the goods with Merve's parents while Merve made their own house liveable. His first priority was hot and cold running water. He bought an old car engine for $15 and mounted a shaft and pulley on it. A centrifugal pump cost another $15, and with a bit of ingenuity, Merve rigged a water system. He bought a hot water tank for the kitchen and put an old storage tank on top of a 30-foot tower to create gravity feed for water. The chimney wasn't in the right place so Merve redesigned the interior and put to use the stone-working skills he had learned from a workmate in Powell River. The new stone fireplace and chimney became a central focus of the house.

With Mary seven months pregnant, Merve was determined to have the house ready for the baby's arrival. Denis was born on May 11, 1936, but Merve was so busy working on the house, he missed the actual birth. Men didn't stay with their wives in those days, but it was customary to show up just before or immediately after the birth.

Understanding that labour would take some time, Merve had dropped Mary off at the Nanaimo hospital and gone back to work. However Mary's labour was unexpectedly brief and easy. Denis arrived minutes before his father got to Mary's bedside. The boy's birth was a happy if slightly overwhelming event for the young parents. Everything had progressed so quickly: their marriage, the move from Powell River, slavishly working to build a home, and now a brand new baby. Thankfully, Denis was a good baby. In Merve's recollection Denis rarely cried.

I don't remember walking the floor with him more than a couple of times and that was when he was teething.

Even though Merve was no longer gainfully employed, he was making more money than he had been in Powell River. The people who had framed the house had left a mass of felled trees from clearing the land. Merve cut them up for firewood. He made two cords a day and sold them for ten dollars a cord.

But there was more to Merve and Mary's days than work. The community offered a rich social life. There was an active Women's Institute, an active Farmer's Institute, and a well-developed co-op movement. Parties and evenings of entertainment were frequent, with a potluck supper dish the usual price of admission. If you had a talent, you displayed it. But social gatherings filled another function as well. It was at the parties in peoples' homes or at the community hall that people found out who needed a helping hand with some project or other, or who might need some advice.

Crime was unheard-of. One time two men held up the gas station in Cassidy. The neighbours turned up, tracked them through the woods, and handed them over to the local police.

Lots of nice things happened. I had arranged to have a man come and plow my garden one day. Well one of his horses went lame and his next-door neighbour, knowing he'd made arrangements, said,

"Here, take my horses. I'm not using them today." And so Jack came and plowed the garden.

No money was expected. But I had a chance to do him a little turn when he had something that needed doing. My garden got in on time and I was able to return the favour.

In 1937, when Denis was a year old, Merve and Mary took a three-week crash course in rural living skills. The program, called Youth Training, was a collaboration between the federal and provincial governments and the University of British Columbia (UBC). Youth Training courses were held across the country. In Nanaimo the Women's Institute and the Farmer's Institute sponsored the program.

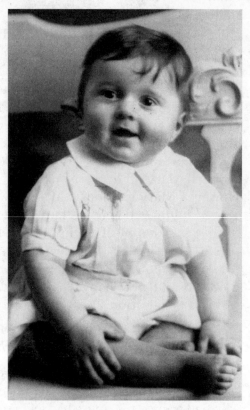

Denis, nine months old, gives daddy Merve a smile.

Merve and Mary loved it. The course taught them all the basics of livestock, horticulture, pruning, the care of poultry, farm mechanics, and blacksmithing. At the end of the program, those who had done well were invited to apply for the eight-week advanced course to be held at the UBC campus in Vancouver.

As soon as Merve and Mary discovered there were living quarters available at UBC, they applied. It was a perfectly logical step. They'd both done particularly well in the three-week course, and here were these 147 acres of beautiful forest that was to provide their livelihood. Merve's plan was to earn a living from a combination of horticulture and poultry farming and he embraced anything that would help him succeed.

They were duly accepted and because they were a married couple with a young child, they were allotted a cabin for housing. Next door lived another young couple from Red Rock in the northern Cariboo who also had a young child. The two women managed to work out a baby-sitting schedule. The occasional help of a student allowed their plan to work so well they never had to miss a class.

Merve thought the course was phenomenal. He and Mary learned it all: dairy farming, butter making, and poultry processing. Many of the classes were held right in the regular university classrooms as part of the diploma curriculum.

It really was an excellent course. They stopped it because of the war and they never picked it up again. They realized they were creating a monster. When these graduates left the course and knew what could be happening in agriculture and what wasn't happening, they pretty well went left of center. The governments, of course, didn't want left of center at that time. Some of these people even went as far as becoming young communists. A lot of them became progressively minded people. There was a lot of good material that came out of those courses. At least some of the graduates went back to their communities and stirred them up in one way or another.

Dr. Paul A. Boving taught the students agriculture, livestock, horticulture, agronomy, and field crops. He was a Dane who had previously taught forestry in his own homeland and the other Scandinavian countries. It was his habit to quiz two or three students each day about their farming plans. "What sort of farm do you have?" "What's the land like?" "What about the climate?" His intention was to steer the students into the sort of farming that would work with their terrain, climate, and location.

When it came his turn, Merve said, "I have 147 acres of old-growth timber on Vancouver Island."

"Good Lord," Dr. Boving said. "You should be taking forestry."

When Dr. Boving offered to send for the Swedish forestry course and tutor Merve, Merve said yes. One lesson that had been instilled in him from boyhood was that opportunities were things to grasp with both hands. You said no only to those things you instinctively knew were not for you. And until you were positive about your path in life, you welcomed new thoughts and new ideas that might shape your future. Learning—all learning—was to be welcomed with open arms.

Two days later, Dr. Boving asked Merve to stay at the end of class. The course in forestry had just come in from the University of

Gothenburg in Sweden, with the small drawback that the entire course was written in Swedish. Merve agreed to pay the $200 fee for the translation and he got down to work.

The Swedish course in forestry was a godsend. There was no English language forestry course available. At the time, the Canadian way of forestry was called "high-grading," which meant you took all the best trees out of the forest and left the poor-quality wood behind. In the United States, in the name of progress, foresters had started clear-cutting. Some Canadians had heard about it and were ready to adopt that method. Merve's Swedish course was founded on a vastly different principle: what you leave in the forest is more important than what you take out. To North Americans the only important thing was what they harvested.

Merve embraced the Swedish method with all his heart and soul. He graduated from the course cognizant of all systems of forestry, including handlogging, which was popular in tropical forests and was also used in parts of British Columbia.

The handloggers worked on the steep slopes and did very well by the forest – better than some others that followed them. They were choosy about the trees they took and they did minimal damage because they felled the trees downhill into the water. Or they would fall them in such a way that they could push them down the hill with jacks on rollers. There were no roads built, and the trees were all within easy reach of the water. They would pick out some of the better trees—in other words, they high-graded but they never destroyed the forests. They could have gone on logging by that method almost forever. They didn't produce great volume but they did produce excellent quality.

Back home at Yellow Point, Merve got serious about planning his own production. He chose to go for single tree selection with occasional group selection of three or four trees where density or disease warranted. It was a system of logging he would use ever after. He took his time assessing before he made that first cut. He looked for trees that were failing and past their prime and marked those. He also noted the trees that were home to eagles and woodpeckers and marked those too—but to keep, not to fall.

At first, Merve cut his trees once every five years because it gave him a harvest big enough to command a decent price at the sawmills.

Marketing and pricing has always been a crook's game in British Columbia. If you market small quantities you're not going to do well. If you market in larger quantities you're going to get much better pricing and much better grading and a much better scale. I was aware of that before I started. A certain amount of volume was necessary if you wanted to get a deal. Over the years, I found that a third of the buyers were crooked. They cheated on scale or grade or volume. You could hold that to a minimum by doing a five-year cut. It works well and has no detrimental effect on the forest ... But it is not as good as cutting annually because with a five-year cut you do tend to take a little more out of the forest at one time. That lets a little more sunlight in and that downgrades the quality of your young growth because they grow too many limbs—they're too bushy.

Merve resolved to start milling his lumber right on the property. He found a man with a mill and the two men co-operated closely, keeping waste to a minimum and practising strict quality control.

It didn't take Merve long to understand the ins and outs of marketing his lumber. The first lesson he learned was the lesson of the "culled log," when his driver delivered a load of logs to the mill and the scaling slip that lists the number of logs, size, and tally came back noting one culled log. Merve knew logs were culled for several reasons: if they were badly rotted, if they were shattered, if they had sporadic faults or rot, or if they had a very bad curve. But Merve also knew that every log in his load was excellent, particularly one very large one with a small chip on the heavy end. The scaling slip didn't mention the size of the cull but it didn't take him long to calculate that the scaler had culled the big log.

When he had another truckload ready to go to the mill, he rode along and got out at the sawmill office.

"Don't take the chains off and don't let them unload until I talk to the scaler," Merve told the driver. Then he walked into the office.

"I'm here to see your scaler," he said to the man at the desk.

"He's out in the yard."

"That's fine. I'll go and see him."

Merve found the scaler standing near his last pile of logs.

"Look, I'm the fellow that sent that load of logs over there," he said by way of introduction, "and I notice here, one cull on that load. I know enough about scaling and grading to know there were no culls on that load. I want that log scaled."

The scaler didn't say a word. He took the slip Merve handed him, walked over to the log, tallied it, and filled in the amount. Merve took the slip back and said, "Now I want the rest of my timber that comes in here scaled on the same basis, and I don't want any more culls. I don't let culls leave the property—I use them for firewood."

Merve had no more culls from that sawmill, but he knew if he'd let that one go, he'd have had a cull on every load he shipped.

Even more significant was the "missing load" syndrome. In Merve's case it happened with a man named George who ran a sawmill. He was an upstanding member of the community, but like so many others, when he found he might get something extra for himself by being a little dishonest, he took the opportunity. At George's mill there was always a missing load. You could never fault him on his scale, and you could never fault him on his price, but if you sent in ten loads you got a cheque for nine. If you sent in twelve loads, you got a cheque for eleven. If you were smart enough to tally your own loads and confront him about it, you'd get your full price. If you didn't, you were out a load.

Merve was lucky. A friend gave him the tip-off about George: "Just drop around the office after you get your cheque and ask about the missing load; then watch what happens. It's very funny."

Sure enough, it was.

The first time Merve shipped to George, he sent eleven loads and got a cheque for ten. The scale was fine, the price was fine, but there was a missing load. So Merve went in to the office.

"George, how about that missing load?"

"There can't be."

"Yes there is. These are the dates when I sent them in."

"Well, it's got to be here somewhere."

George turned into a cyclone. He tore through the office, tossing papers everywhere, and then, sure enough, right at the edge of the desk, directly above the wastebasket, was the missing slip. He looked shocked. "Sorry about that," he said and brought out the chequebook. "It won't happen again."

Three weeks later, Merve was back in George's office. "George, how about that missing load?" And Merve watched the same performance.

Remembering the favour his friend had done, Merve tipped off another fellow, Clarence Wager. Merve had done Wager's bucking for him. By this time, Merve was pretty good at estimating board feet so he told Clarence that he had about 28,000 board feet to ship to George. He also told him what to expect.

Clarence called him up after the delivery and said, "Merve, you were out on that amount of wood—you were about 10,000 feet out."

"Whose truck did you have?"

Clarence told him the truck and told him he'd hauled four loads. Merve figured it out. The truck's capacity was 7,000 feet. Four loads meant 28,000 feet.

"The next time you're in town, go in to see George," Merve advised. "And tell him you want the missing load. You'll get a kick out of what happens."

Clarence went into town the next day. At about two o'clock he called Merve. Clarence was laughing so hard he could barely talk. "I went in and did what you said. It sounded awful crazy to me, but you've never given me a bum steer yet so I thought I'd do it. It was well worth it. The circus act that took place in that office!"

"I know exactly what you mean," Merve said. "But he found the slip?"

"Yep—and it tallied up to 28,500 feet."

✲ ✲ ✲

When Merve started his logging operation, all sorts of buyers made their way to his door with offers for the standing timber. There were bona fide offers and there were offers that were crooked. Merve had no trouble weeding out the good from the bad. But his reply was the same to them all: thanks but no thanks.

> One chap, having found out that I'd paid $1,500 for the property, came along and offered me $1,500 cash. He said, "This reimburses you for your property completely. I get the timber and you keep the land." By this time I'd done a bit of evaluating of my own timber and I said, "Thanks, that's a bona fide offer, but I'm not the least bit interested. For one thing, I'm not interested in complete liquidation and I'm not interested in getting $1,500, investing it, and making a pile of money. I'm going to cut my own timber."
>
> "Too bad," the man said. "You'll never get a better offer."

When Merve did his first cut, he was pleased with the result. It paid a good return, but it also gave him the satisfaction of knowing he'd made a cut, yet when he looked out the window he couldn't be sure where he'd made it. The deer were still gliding through the trees, the grouse were sitting on the stumps, and the other birds and animals seemed happy enough. He had some money in the bank and a roof over his head. Why cut it all?

Merve made a second cut and then came another offer. A Mr. Cowan had bought the timber next to Merve's place and he wanted Merve's trees as well. Merve refused the offer and told Cowan why.

"You're a smart man," Cowan said. "You have chosen a way of life that you can't buy with dollars. You and your wife have chosen contentment and you can't buy that. You can buy excitement, but you can't buy contentment. More credit to you. I won't bother you again, but if you ever do want to sell your timber, please contact me."

Cowan turned to leave, then stopped as a thought came to him. "By the way," he said. "You live on the lake here. I'm going to be setting a mill up on the lake, and we're going to tow the logs in to the mill with a small boat. Would you like to run the powerboat for me? Your time is your own and you could be available a couple of times a week—that's all we need. If you'd like to work for me, that would be fine—no strings attached."

"Sure, Mr. Cowan. I'd be delighted."

Merve got four dollars an hour to run the powerboat. He loved being on the water and he liked messing around with boats. On top of that he was getting a regular monthly paycheque of about $75, which was a fair wage for what he was doing. It was a good arrangement.

Meanwhile Merve was still in touch with the friends he'd made at UBC. Out of that friendship had sprung a society called Rural Youth in Training. The society's purpose was to keep the learning alive. The students went back to their homes in Prince Rupert, the Fraser Valley, the Okanagan, the Queen Charlottes, the Peace River, Vancouver Island, and all points in the province with a strong desire to inspire other young people in the province.

One of them hit upon the idea of writing columns in the newspapers. No paper was interested, but then one of the youths said, "I know Mr. Hayden, the editor of *Country Life in B.C.* I bet he'd be interested in this."

Sure enough, he was. He replied to their query by return post. "Yes, I'd be most interested. That's one section of my paper that I feel is weak and I haven't known who to contact. I'd be very happy if your little organization would take over a page for young people in my publication every month."

Merve was elected editor of the page, which suited him just fine. He'd enjoyed literature immensely in school and this was a wonderful creative outlet. Merve edited the page for three years— and it was directly as a result of that job that he stumbled into one of the most embarrassing and humiliating moments of his life.

Unbeknownst to this small B.C. youth group, three similar groups had sprung up in other provinces across the country. The CBC found the idea interesting enough to build a radio show around it. They contacted a representative from each of the groups to come and be on the show. Merve was their contact in B.C. The format of the show was a debate in which each young person delivered a brief presentation, idea, or purpose; then the discussion was open to debate.

When the production manager of the show in Vancouver called Merve with the invitation, Merve said yes. He liked talking to groups and saw this as a marvellous opportunity to get some really good ideas across. He worked hard at his presentation, and on the morning of the show he hopped an early ferry to Vancouver to give himself plenty of time. The production manager at the studio was a genial man who put Merve completely at ease in a dress rehearsal. He set Merve up in a sealed and windowless booth with two chairs, a table, and a microphone. The producer sat down opposite and Merve began his speech. He sailed through the rehearsal.

"You've done a superb job," the producer told him. "That's great. If it goes over like that on the air, I'll be really pleased." He was so confident in Merve that he left him alone in the booth with the instructions to simply listen to his earphone and start his speech again on cue.

Merve sat alone in the square box with the microphone as his only audience. He listened on his earphones, heard the show's preamble, and then his cue: "You're on!"

For the first time in my life I hit the panic button. I made an awful mess of what I was trying to say. I couldn't concentrate. It seemed to me so utterly futile to be sitting there talking to a piece of equipment … that was one time when I lost all track of what I wanted to say— I blanked out. I felt like a fool for weeks. I almost wished I could press a button and obliterate myself.

When Merve bought his 147 acres, it was a beautiful piece of wild forest, utterly untouched by man. It was typical of coastal Vancouver Island with trees of all sizes and ages growing on the land. All the native species were there: fir, cedar, hemlock, balsam, arbutus, alder, maple, crabapple, aspen, juniper, yew, and one vine maple that proved an eternal puzzle. Vine maples are common in the Interior and on the Mainland coast but very rare on Vancouver Island.

He couldn't walk across the land without encountering five or six deer. Every species of bird from the largest bald eagle to the tiniest rufous hummingbird nested in the trees. The forest was their home. The land supported every kind of wildlife and every sort of bug and insect. Worms crawled over the ground when it rained and burrowed under the soil when the sun shone. It was just like the land he had grown up on, so it felt like home. As he walked through his forest he was at peace with himself and his fellow man. To him it was as close as he could get to a Garden of Eden.

But when he thought about making a living on this land, Merve didn't think about forestry. The thought of a sustainable living forest was the last thing on his mind. He thought about agriculture. It wasn't until he had completed the Swedish forestry course that he really saw what a treasure he had: not farmland but a precious piece of temperate rain forest that had the potential to sustain him and his family for the rest of his life. The sustainable selective system of forestry Merve learned was completely new to Canada but had been used successfully in Europe for hundreds of years. And if the system didn't work, he figured he could make a living by other means. He could build a house out of the trees growing on the land. He could grow his own food and fuel. He could keep chickens and a cow. And he could shoot the abundant deer for meat.

Merve made his living from the forest that first year by cutting up firewood. He simply cut up all the trees he'd had to take down to clear land for his building site. He wasted nothing, and he enjoyed the work; it was physically tiring but stress-free. Earning a living from cutting firewood was all the proof Merve needed to know he and Mary could make a living on the land.

By making this choice to save the forest he called "Wildwood," Merve unsuspectingly created a unique forest that—several decades later—would become an icon, an outdoor classroom that would host foresters from around the world and schoolchildren by the thousands.

Throughout the forest it is difficult to discern where logging has taken place. Wildwood includes a riparian area, or swamp (below), which both preserves moisture and shelters wildlife. It produces insects such as flies and mosquitoes that birds feed on. Bears come here to eat the skunk cabbage roots. "These are zones in our forest that must be very carefully protected and not worked in with large equipment," Merve says.

The technical crew cut him off and plugged in another speaker. Merve was off the show. In later years, Merve realized it was a good object lesson. At the time, however, he was painfully embarrassed.

The producer realized immediately what had happened and apologized. "I should have stayed in the booth with you."

"No, it was my fault," Merve said.

"Well, maybe it was both our faults," the producer said.

Several things came out of that botched-up performance, not the least of which was a profound sympathy for anyone caught up in the experience of stage fright. Years later, when remembering the incident and the reason for it, his appreciation for the initiative of Canadian youth was reinforced.

Apparently the program was quite successful. It stirred up quite a bit of interest in youth activity across the country. After a few years it wound down. It's my feeling that it's long past time that we got our young people out front instead of all these nitwits we have at the head of different organizations – get some of our young people out in front. They have the ideas that can do something for the world. The others are living in the past and unfortunately we haven't buried that past.

It's time we stopped looking at the so-called heroes of the past. Some of them are … I don't want to detract from the people that are outstanding. There are outstanding people … but too many only think they are. We've got to get rid of them somehow.

Chapter 8

Co-operative and Guerilla Movements

Life in Yellow Point was idyllic. Merve and Mary worked hard at what they loved to do. They had each other, their young son, and a growing circle of good friends. They had a feeling of security they'd never experienced in Powell River, where they had never been sure whether Merve's card would be in the rack or pulled when he came to punch in.

They were short of cash at times, but so was everyone at one time or another. They were ambitious, too, and set their sights high. When Denis was old enough to go to school, Mary decided to go back to teaching so that Merve could free himself up to do some work on the house. Each morning Mary and Denis would go off together on the school bus and come home the same way in the afternoon.

Merve worked on their house, harvested his timber, and picked up odd jobs in the neighbourhood. He cut wood, felled trees for people, and made poles and fence posts from the thinnings on his property. But his main job was to turn their house into a really beautiful and comfortable home.

We had innumerable friends. Every weekend there was someone here. The people who came were often practical, so quite frequently they'd end up giving you a hand. Then you'd do something in return for them. And so we had a lot of mutual help and solid friendships. It was really quite an idyllic life in many ways.

Merve's early experiences as a forester shaped many of his ideas and a good deal of his philosophy. His parents had instilled in him a sense of responsibility and duty to his community. He believed being involved was the right thing to do. He joined the ratepayers association and the local activity club. The political philosophy of the Co-operative Commonwealth Federation (CCF) also attracted him, so he joined the local executive. It was the word "Co-operative" that he identified with.

The original concept was that people would own more of their resources through co-operative ventures. When Tommy Douglas in Saskatchewan formed the first CCF government in Canada, he immediately appointed a Minister of Co-operatives. Douglas felt that the government shouldn't be involved in the setting up of co-operatives, but it should be in the business of making the setting up of them feasible and legislatively correct. In other words, opening the doors and laying down a red carpet to the idea. They let people do it on their own with their own ideas, initiatives, and purposes.

In 1942, Merve had good reason to get behind the co-operative movement. That was the year he had the opportunity to buy another 100 acres of virgin timber adjacent to his own land. For Merve, that 100 acres represented complete self-sufficiency and he went to his banker to borrow the $800 he needed for the purchase. He had clear title to his property but no money in the bank. The banker told Merve that wasn't good enough. He could not lend money on land as collateral. Bonds were acceptable security but land was not.

"If I had bonds," Merve said to him, "you'd get them dumped on your desk so fast it would make your head spin."

"You mean you would sacrifice gilt-edged securities as collateral?"

"That's right."

The banker and Merve exchanged a few more clipped words and Merve left. He wasn't the only one who had been turned down by the bank and he wasn't the only one who'd had enough. That local group of fed-up people got together and decided to form a credit union. It wasn't a new concept. Credit unions had been operating for a hundred years in other countries and were becoming known in Canada. They were being organized by local people with a board of directors drawn from the group of members who were then responsible to the other members. It was the kind of co-operative venture that appealed to Merve.

He and his friends wasted no time organizing the Nanaimo and District Credit Union and the Ladysmith Credit Union. By the time the Nanaimo and District Credit Union was up and running, the 100-acre parcel was gone. The credit union came too late to help Merve, but it did immeasurable good for countless others.

Six months after Merve had walked out of the bank, he ran into the bank manager.

"I haven't seen you in my bank lately," he said.

"No—and you won't see me," Merve said.

"Well where are you doing your banking?"

"I belong to the credit union."

"You mean you've left a good, standard bank to go with a bunch of amateur bankers?"

"They're only amateur to the extent that they're 150 years old," Merve replied. "I don't think that's quite amateur."

The banker paused and studied Merve. "You know," he said, "I've thought about that proposition that you came in with. I was foolish. I could have given you that money myself as a personal loan. I often wish I had. You were right. The value of timber has been going up steadily ever since."

"Well, it's too late now," Merve said. "The timber's gone and you've lost one customer for life."

The need for the credit union was greater than anyone had anticipated. It formed so quickly it caught several people off guard. Merve would have been a charter member, but he was speaking to a group in Ladysmith the night the charter was signed. The founding group was holding an information meeting that night when they realized there was nothing left to talk about; it was time to get on with it and sign the charter right then.

Merve served on the executive in various capacities and showed a clear vision for what lay ahead. At one meeting, Merve had said, "I'll stay on the executive until we have ten million dollars in assets."

"Well, you must plan on staying around for a long time, Merve," a fellow member shot back.

Two years later, the credit union's assets topped ten million dollars, and true to his word, Merve resigned.

The credit union prospered. People flocked in to deposit money. But no one was taking out loans, and so the credit union was in danger of becoming the victim of its own success. Without loans there were no earnings, and therefore no dividends to the members.

Something had to be done. One night the board came up with a scheme. They would all put their names into a hat and the one whose name was drawn would have to take out a loan. That would allow the credit union to advertise the fact that loans were being issued and the idea might motivate others to do the same.

The board agreed it was a fine idea. They put their names into the hat and drew out Merve's name. He was a bit nonplussed but they had had an agreement, so he took out a loan for $200.

Merve got home that evening and, as usual, Mary had a cup of tea ready for him.

"A funny thing happened at the meeting tonight," Merve said as he settled into his chair. "I took out the first loan on the books."

"Well what for?" Mary cried. "We don't need a loan. Now we'll just be in debt!"

"Well, now wait a minute," Merve said. "You've been talking about wanting a new dress and a new sewing machine. Take the $200 and go out and buy them."

Suddenly the loan didn't seem so bad. It did the same thing for the board members as it did for Mary. When they asked him what he was going to do with the money, Merve told them about the new sewing machine and possibly some new tools for himself. Loan applications started rolling in, the credit union started making money, and the members began to see their faith in the idea pay off. Merve became more convinced than ever that co-operative ventures were the way to go.

> *A lot of people today don't realize that there's a lot of things they could do to help themselves and be much more independent and less debt-ridden if they would work together—if they would pool their interests and pool their wealth. But they're told they should be individuals. Well, an individual is very vulnerable. He's like an individual chicken that's prey to a hawk. An individual person is prey to the pirates of society, and we have plenty of them. When people get together and decide to do something as a group rather than as individuals, they can really do wonderful things. It is not necessary to have big business and big industry and big executives do things for you—people together can do it much more effectively and efficiently and accomplish more in the long run.*

While Merve learned about co-operation, he and Mary also discovered self-sufficiency. The neighbourhood activities club promoted agriculture and gardening and held demonstrations in various gardening and handicraft activities. Mary became adept at spinning, weaving, and dyeing. She and Merve undertook a joint project with wool dyeing. Using only natural materials from their own land, they produced 54 different colours. The only colour they could not produce was blue, but they created a gorgeous green. From the root of the Oregon grape plants they produced a vibrant canary yellow that was so powerful even the sun couldn't fade it. The bark of the elder tree produced a full, rich brown.

> *We had a lot of fun learning to live off the land. We were still feeling the effects of the Depression, and people were concerned with how to maintain themselves, so the knowledge did them well. It meant that a lot of things that they normally would have had to buy, they could simply produce themselves. And they had a lot of satisfaction from doing it. To be able to do something—your own feeling of achievement and the knowledge that you've done something worthwhile that can be passed on to someone else—is a tremendous builder of character. It makes people feel they have real value and that they have something to contribute and that they have a place in the scheme of things.*

Merve was almost 30 years old when the Second World War broke out. While many people had been ignoring the warning signs, others knew it was coming. Merve could see the inevitable. He was not interested in soldiering, but he was no pacifist either. He couldn't imagine sitting down and waiting for the inevitable. But he was working in the woods, and because timber was an essential commodity there was no chance he'd be called up. Merve was not about to volunteer, but at the same time he knew in his heart that Hitler and Mussolini would have to be stopped.

When the Japanese jumped into the war, the issue came close to home. The west coast of North America and Vancouver Island were vulnerable to attack. The Japanese could land there easily. Self-defense became a necessity and self-defense was something Merve could get behind whole-heartedly.

> *You're not going out to hit somebody over the head or try to take something away from them or harm them or rape their women. But you are determined not to let somebody walk in and do those things to you.*

He and other men in the area, including many who had served in the First World War, recognized that it was time to get some training. They formed a guerilla unit called the Pacific Coast Militia Rangers. Word about the Rangers spread until quite a few were ready to turn it into a formal unit. But they were very clear that their concern was with the Japanese Army—not the Japanese people.

Most of us had known Japanese and liked them. They had been on the coast here for some time and they were fine citizens and they didn't like their home country's attitude any more than we did. But they were suspect and they were hauled away by the Canadian government. Actually it was criminal what they did to the Japanese. It was almost as bad as what the Japanese did to other people [in their prisoner-of-war camps].

The army put pilings up on Long Beach to prevent the Japanese from landing. A Japanese submarine came in as far as Point Estevan at the tip of rugged Hesquiat Peninsula at the north end of Clayoquot Sound on the west coast of Vancouver Island. Some claimed that a Japanese submarine fired on the lighthouse on June 20, 1942. Whether or not the rumour was true, forming and training the unit took on a sense of urgency.

The army agreed and Brigadier Roy Sargent at Camp Nanaimo made the drill hall available for the first assembly of the militia. He saw it as an opportunity for them to get organized and to establish leadership. Merve remembers the commander of the camp as an excellent fellow.

He was one militarist who you could point to and say, there's a man who believes he's serving his country. He does it with honour and distinction, and yet he's a civilian in this respect: he respects all people's feelings and all people's integrity.

The army had already decided who was going to command this civilian rabble: a man from Duncan named Thorne. As a major in the First World War he had served with distinction, but in civilian life he'd developed a great fondness for alcohol and had recently begun to hit the bottle heavily.

The night Thorne was supposed to come and take command in the Nanaimo drill hall, he was sitting in a beer parlour in Duncan unable to get up. Time passed and the men started to get impatient, including the brigadier.

A logger from Duncan knew where Thorne was but diplomatically said, "Oh, he's unavoidably delayed."

Finally the door opened and a group of men from Lake Cowichan (near Duncan) entered the restless room. They had stopped at the beer parlour too.

"Any sign of Thorne?" someone asked.

"He's drunker than a skunk in Duncan. He'll never get here tonight."

Pandemonium broke out. They stomped their feet, catcalled, whistled, and then one man with his wits about him yelled, "I nominate Captain Stronach to take charge of this!"

Captain Stronach had also fought in the First World War. He'd been in the engineers and was much decorated for his bravery and his ingenuity. There couldn't have been a better fit.

"I second the motion!" another voice yelled above the crowd. "All in favour raise your hands."

Hands, including Merve Wilkinson's, shot up all around the room. Order was restored, and possibly for the first time in Canadian history a Canadian officer was elected by a show of hands. Merve was standing near the brigadier and overheard him say: "Great! That's the way to go!"

Stronach took it all in stride. He stepped up to the front and said, "Thank you, men. Now, we've got to sort ourselves out. We're not going to be in one unit. We'll break down into units for our respective areas." He proceeded to sort the men out. Within minutes he had over 30 units gathered around the room with instructions to elect a leader from among themselves—a man who they could trust and respect. Within an hour, the nucleus of the Pacific Coast Rangers was set up and ready for training.

The Rangers became an effective unit. They didn't have to fight a war, but they were called on to fight forest fires and to handle other local problems. They also assisted in army exercises, taking a defensive role so that the new army recruits could practise. The recruits—mostly from downtown Montreal, Toronto, and Vancouver—didn't stand a chance against the locals, who had been living in the woods all their lives.

On their first defensive exercise, Stronach and his Rangers were asked to hold Crystal Lake, a beautiful body of water nestled in the wilderness behind Mount Benson, the mountain that looms over Nanaimo. They were to hold the area against a hypothetical attack from a Japanese force. Merve was a second-class signalman.

It was in November. We went out the night before and it was good training in how to keep yourself warm and dry in the middle of a rainy, wet, miserable night and be ready to go into action at dawn. The exercise was officially supposed to start at 0800 hours.

Charlie Stronach and the main force were down near the lake and he had them spread around in such a way that he knew he had a pretty good chance of defending it. He had scout packs out on the surrounding mountainsides to keep an eye out for where the army would come from. He figured they'd come the easy way—which they did. There was a good road to the north. But he wasn't taking any chances.

My little group—we were about fifteen strong—were on the shoulder of Wolf Mountain. We could read the signals of the group on Mount Benson's shoulder and they could read the signalman down at the lake and so on.

Stronach sent scouts out in all directions and he sent them out at dawn. The scouts who went north came across the army headquarters. The army had moved in overnight and set up just as we had. But the guards had been up all night and were so sleepy that our men grabbed them, gagged them, and exchanged uniforms with them. They took the army rifles and left their own behind and went right into headquarters. I don't know just how they got into the commander's tent, but they did get in and said, "The jig's up. You're captured."

The army headquarters was captured by eight backwoods rabble and the commander was furious.

Meanwhile, Merve was up on the mountain watching for semaphore signals. The first signalman down in the valley was a local eye doctor. His message flashed up to Merve: "Report to Headquarters. Enemy Captured."

Merve read it. "What on earth?" He signalled back: "Please repeat."

"Report to Headquarters. Enemy Captured."

Merve turned around and said to his team, "Well, it's over."

"But we haven't seen anybody yet!"

"It's over. I just got a signal from the doc on the other side and he wouldn't miscue. This has got to be authentic."

By the time Merve and his boys got down off their post on Wolf Mountain, the army commander and his staff were in "handcuffs" with a guard on them—and they were mad as hell, or actually madder. The colonel was livid. "This was not supposed to start until 0800 hours. You guys came in at 0630."

"The Japanese don't operate on our schedules," said Charlie Stronach.

The colonel demanded a hearing at Camp Nanaimo. A court-martial would have suited him just fine.

Brigadier Roy Sargent was in his office when the entire troop came marching in: the captured army, the Rangers, the commanders, everyone.

The army colonel started: "This man started the exercise an hour-and-a-half early and…" He continued to tell what happened.

The brigadier listened to the colonel and said, "Captain Stronach, do you have something to say?"

"Yes sir, I have. We are a guerilla unit. The Japanese are not an army that runs on Canadian schedules or on any army schedules except their own. I took action appropriate to what I thought was right in defending my assignment. I ascertained from where the army was going to attack. I gave my scouts orders to act with discretion and care but to take any action they thought might be necessary. I have every confidence in their corporal as a man of judgment."

Sargent leaned forward and rested his arms on his desk. "Congratulations, Captain Stronach," he said. "We need more of this kind of initiative in the armed forces. Extraordinarily well done! Thank you, sir!"

At the end of the war, the Rangers disbanded and the men went back to fishing, farming, mining, logging, and all the things they'd done before they'd prepared for the possibility of a Japanese attack.

Merve went back to working in his community—logging his land on a five-year basis and gradually doing more and more small contracting work.

Chapter 9

Community and Family Values

In the years right after the war, life was busy for Merve and his family—so busy that they didn't take too much notice when Mary started to develop headaches. At the beginning she didn't think anything of them. She chalked them up to tiredness. She would take an aspirin and lie down or have a cup of tea and eventually the headache would go away. Over time they became more and more severe and more persistent. But Mary coped because she was too busy to take time out.

Merve was busy too. His building business was thriving and he was able to choose which jobs he wanted to do. Gradually, he began to swing over to stonework as a preference. He had a loyal clientele who hired him to do all their maintenance work and small building projects. The building business was a tremendous help to the family income and improved their standard of living considerably. The forest accounted for one-fifth of Merve's working time and gave him one-third of his income. The development of his land was done. The roads were in. Merve settled into a routine of cutting on the basis of an annual growth rate and growing his building business.

There was hardly a person in Yellow Point that Merve didn't know and there was hardly a person he knew who didn't become a teacher for him in some way.

They were a vast variety of people and they were good, solid people. Both Mary and I had a lot of friends amongst them. Mary had a good many friends amongst the women, especially the elderly women. And as we lived here, I began to look at my community and think, "What makes this community tick the way it does?" There were such a variety of individuals but there was something there that was a driving force that meant the community worked together very well. You never heard of any crime—it was almost not thought of.

What I did notice was that there were some people who, in minor ways, were more successful than others both in their own lives and in their relationships with their neighbours. And this success helped them to accumulate what they wanted and needed, not in extravagant amounts, but in sufficient quantity that you could say they were the more well-off people in the community.

And I began to think, "What is it about these people that makes them successful?" What I noticed was that the most successful people were the people with the highest ethical attitude toward their neighbours. They were the people whose handshake was better than a written contract. They functioned on their word and they stood behind what they believed to be right.

One of Merve's "successful people" was a cattle dealer by the name of Joe Ham. He and his wife made a good living. He knew stock exceedingly well and he was known as an honest horse trader. If you went to Joe Ham and told him you wanted a cow and told him you didn't know a darn thing about cows but you wanted a good producer—or you knew nothing about horses, you just wanted a quiet, steady horse—then the animal you got from him was the right animal for you. Joe Ham would not overcharge—with one exception: if he was dealing with another cattle dealer, and that went double if the other fellow was a bit shady. He delighted in outwitting other cattle dealers but in being scrupulously honest with the public. He had his own code of ethics.

In Merve's opinion Hedley Vickers was one of the outstanding men in the community. He was a well-educated English gentleman who was an art collector and an avid livestock fancier. He raised beautiful registered Jerseys—prize winners every one of them. Next door to Hedley lived two homesteaders. They were coal miners from the North of England who had very distinct accents: "you" became "you'm" and "we" became "we'm" and so on. These two bachelors were building themselves a home and a barn. They weren't really farmers but they wanted to be self-sufficient.

Meat was pretty difficult to come by in the summer. There were no deep freezers and no refrigerators and precious little ice. But there was so much wild meat at that time—deer by the hundreds—that a lot of people depended on it. As long as you weren't abusing the privilege, the game warden didn't see you take the odd deer for Sunday dinner. Real poaching and pit lamping were frowned upon.

One hot summer day, these two miners were complaining to their fellow workers about the lack of fresh meat.

"No fresh meat?" one of the other miners asked incredulously. "There are deer all over your place every night. Take your pit lamp and go out and get yourself one. It's the easiest way. Turn on your light and when you see a pair of eyes, shoot. You can practically walk right up to the animal, so there's nothing to it."

It sounded like a good idea. The field next to the miners' homestead belonged to Hedley Vickers and he happened to have a bunch of heifers out there. So the miners went out the next night with their light, and they didn't have to go very far before they saw a pair of eyes. Of course the eyes belonged to one of Hedley's heifers, but the men didn't know that in the dark and they shot it dead.

Hedley heard the shot and jumped out of bed. He was pretty sure he had a pit-lamper in his yard. He threw on his robe and slipped out the front door just in time to hear the argument.

"Now we'm did it!"

"What do you mean we'm did it? You'm pulled the trigger!"

"Yeah, but we'm were here! We'm went hunting for meat so we'm did it!"

The argument waxed eloquent. It was even touching on the code of British law that stated an accomplice to the crime was equally guilty, when Hedley could no longer contain himself. He stepped forward. "Now boys, I don't really care whether you'm or we'm shot my heifer. The animal is worth $250 and you can pay me $250 and the animal is yours. Whether you'm or we'm eats the meat, I don't care." He could have called the police and had the pair arrested. The men would have been fined at least $500. But Hedley was a fair man. These men were his next-door neighbours. They knew $250 was a fair price and Hedley knew the men had learned their lesson.

The lessons Merve learned from the people in his community came to rest on a strong foundation. They were a continuation of the lessons he'd learned in childhood. His parents had taught Merve right from wrong—and they continued to do so.

Dad and Mom continued to pass on their knowledge—their codes of conduct and ethics and so on. They didn't try to push me into anything. But they let me know what they felt was the right way to go. We were close in the respect that we lived very close and that we were close as individuals. There was a real bond of affection between us.

Throughout the community was a great sharing of knowledge and principles from one generation to the other. This cohesiveness continued until the 1960s, when decline set in and families began to break apart.

William and Christina,
Christmas 1949.

The family was a family unit three times a day on weekends and holidays and two times a day the rest of the time. You sat down together at mealtimes and talked about the things that you were interested in. Mom and Dad would laugh and joke or caution you. There was no TV with all its crazy nonsense to distract young minds into thinking that crime is essential— that you go around hitting people over the head, or you go roaring around in automobiles, or that you steal airplanes to escape from something or other.

I can remember the radio as being a very valuable instrument in helping me to broaden myself and my knowledge and understanding. In the 1930s I listened to Hitler and Mussolini and Churchill and Roosevelt and all these prominent figures. We listened to them speak and were able to formulate our own opinions of what they were like. These were not public relations opinions. We got the goods. Commentators went to work on what they had said—that was fine— but they didn't tell you ahead of time what the speaker was going to say. They listened to the speeches and then they tore them apart. Some of them were really good at analyzing a speech and giving not just one perspective, but two or three possible interpretations. You had a spectrum of information based on accuracy, authenticity, and honesty. Today we have information based on corruption, duplicity, and downright lies.

Merve's world was a world where basic honesty was worth more than money. People were considerate of each other and worked together. These people practised today's almost cliché phrase, "It takes a whole village to raise a child." If a child needed guidance or correction, any adult felt free to do it and nobody objected. If a child was scolded by an adult and came home to tell the tale, they were likely to get another scolding because the parent was confident their child had had a talking-to for a very good reason. If a child was naughty, he might get his ears cuffed or he might get a quick whack on the backside.

Denis with a nice catch of fish, 1949.

I know that Denis got a swat on the butt at least once. Not a severe one but it stung a bit. Kids want you to be firm. First, they want you to give them good guidance. They want to be able to come to you and ask you what is right and wrong and to be told simply and to the point. They want to know how far they can go. They're experimenting and thank the Lord they are! Otherwise no progress is made; nothing is done if you're not experimenting. But young people want authority. They want it to be kind and they want to know it comes from someone who loves them. And if it's a stranger, they want it to come from someone who regards them as a person.

In the '30s, '40s, and '50s a two-job family was rare. Mom or Dad was home with the kids. They were home to teach them the skills they would need. My experience with young people is that they love it if you take the time to show them, and it makes the difference between their becoming useful citizens or something society wants to get rid of. It's not the young peoples' fault—it's the fault of their parents and the forces of society. There may be the odd bad apple but I think they are so few as to be a total rarity.

Once, on a club canoe trip, a young six-year-old came with his parents. The boy was known as a holy terror. In Merve's opinion the parents didn't have a highly functioning relationship with either their son or each other. But he could see that Tim was a bright little boy.

When it came time to camp on the first night, Merve gathered firewood to cook the evening meal. He'd just lit it and got it going when young Tim got a stick and scattered the fire all over the ground.

Merve sat Tim down. "Look, Tim, that was stupid and I don't think you are stupid. That's the fire we were going to cook our dinner on. Now you've spoiled it and you'll have to wait an extra half hour for your dinner—just like the rest of us."

The next morning, Merve got up early to get the fire going. Tim was up too.

"How are you this morning, Tim?"

"Oh great, Mr. Wilkinson."

"Now, Tim, you're going to light the fire this morning."

Tim's eyes got big and round. "Can I?"

"Yes," Merve said. "And I'm going to show you how."

Merve got some firewood. He showed Tim how to make shavings and how to use a little bit of pitch from a tree. Then he handed Tim a match. Tim's eyes glowed as brightly as the fire.

Tim lit every fire from then on for the rest for the trip. He did the job well and he caused no more trouble. Even his mother noticed a change. On the third night of the trip as everyone was sitting around the campfire, she said, "I don't know what's happened to Timmy. He's been such a good little boy."

Merve was sitting opposite Timmy, just across the fire. He caught the boy's eye and they exchanged a big wink and a grin.

Tim spent a lot of time at Merve's place after that, and he always made himself useful. He had a lot of initiative, energy, and enthusiasm. Merve kept track of him until he graduated from high school.

After that he was going off to take a job, and I think he's done well. He just needed someone to do something with him—to show him how and explain and recognize him as a person. He was young and eager and wanting to learn. He needed guidance—that and the feeling that he was respected and loved.

★ ★ ★

Meanwhile, Denis was growing up into a fine young man. Like Merve, he was an only child. They wanted more children, but the doctor who had attended Mary's birth had bungled the job. And although that could have been reversed, there was a bigger difficulty.

Merve had had a minor illness he'd put down to swollen glands. When he finally went to his doctor for tests, he found out he was sterile. The "minor" illness had turned out to be mumps, and sterility was not an uncommon side effect. Merve and Mary talked about adopting, and then Mary began getting the headaches.

Like Merve, Denis was never lonely. The Wilkinson home was open to all the neighbourhood kids. Denis had a lot of friends that he always felt free to invite over for the day or the weekend. He visited his friends' homes too, but more often than not the Wilkinson home, with its warm welcome and ready opportunities for catching fish, was a big attraction.

Like Merve when he was a boy, Denis and his friends were also expected to make themselves useful. They were only too glad to help because Merve gave them the biggest treat a twelve- or thirteen-year-old boy could wish for: driving lessons in his truck.

> *It was an old truck I used for hauling things around the place. It didn't have a licence on it but there were a lot of old logging roads that hooked up to my logging roads, so they could drive the interior section of Yellow Point with this truck.*
>
> *In return for me letting them drive the truck and teaching them to drive, they would haul in my wood. All I had to do was cut a bunch of wood and say, "Hey kids, I've got some wood to bring in." "Oh, okay where's it at? We'll get it right away!"*

One day the boys took the truck way up back into the bush. Suddenly Merve saw it coming out so fast he couldn't believe his eyes. The truck was taking the incline at 35 mph when 15 mph should have been the maximum. They'd heard a cougar scream.

> *If you've ever heard a cougar scream, there's nothing in the world like it. I've heard it twice, and both times it lifted my hat. Your hair literally does go on end. It sounds like, I don't know what ... like a demented person being murdered and hacked up with an axe. It's just a horrible sound.*

A few weeks later, Merve was hunting in the same area. The cougar was a good half-mile away from Merve when he heard it. His hat lifted right up.

The boys didn't go back to that area of the woods for weeks after the cougar incident. But Merve taught them what to do in a cougar encounter. The important thing, he said, is don't bend over.

Stay erect. A man is not normal prey. If you're bending over, you're a four-footed animal and that is normal prey.

When Denis and his friends entered their early teens they started looking for ways to use up their excess energy. Merve suggested a junior drama club, and about 22 boys and girls joined up. They were full of energy and enthusiasm, and so was Merve.

They decided to put on two performances annually, each performance consisting of three one-act plays. Merve directed and drew his assistants from among the club members. The plays were invariably a sell-out. The junior drama club flourished for four years, often taking part in junior drama festivals and enjoying a great deal of success. They came away from one festival with a best actress award, a second-best male actor, and top honours for the stage director. At another festival, the group came away with second-best supporting actress, best technical producer, and second place overall.

So our little group had something to feel proud about. And you know, it's interesting, I meet some of those kids from time to time. They come and introduce themselves and they say, "You wouldn't remember me. I was in the drama club, I'm so and so." And right away I know them. The ones I know of and have kept track of—every one has turned out to be a really good, solid citizen. Some of them are very progressive in their fields—people of whom we can be proud in our society. I feel that the sort of disciplinary work they did when they were that age helped them to turn out well.

After four years the kids grew out of the junior drama club and the group disbanded. Some of the young people went on to join the Yellow Point Drama Group, which was flourishing under the direction of Ann Mossman, a fierce Scots woman loved by some and feared by others. She was an excellent director and drama teacher and added much to that amateur theatre group's reputation.

After finishing his first cut in 1945, Merve looked around at what he had done and liked what he saw. Not only was the forest intact and as beautiful as ever, but also that cut returned to him all the money he had invested in the property. It also paid back the cost of building the road, and covered his wages as well.

The first cut had done nothing more than thin the forest. Wildwood still contained its great old granddaddy trees, its trees of every size and kind, and even its tiny year-old trees, struggling to get enough light so they could grow. It was those youngest trees that really flourished, welcoming the removal of the tall trees that had been depriving them of sunshine.

The forest was still there. Merve removed no more trees from his land for five years, and during that time he marvelled at how quickly the forest filled back in. If a person visited the forest a year after the first cut, the only evidence of logging they could find was the odd stump scattered here and there. He was pleased with his work.

Although Merve knew without doubt that Wildwood should not be used as strictly agricultural land, he also knew that he could combine agriculture with forestry. The land would also support a wonderful garden and orchard, a cow, and some chickens. In fact the livestock augmented the deer and helped them keep the underbrush and small trees in balance. By adding domestic cattle into the woodland mix, Merve had, in effect, returned the elk to the land. Cows feed much like the wild elk that used to roam that part of Vancouver Island.

After his second cut in 1951 Merve's enthusiasm for sustainable forestry stretched beyond the bounds of his own land. Merve liked to talk to people and he didn't mind telling them what he was

doing. People became curious. A few of the curious wanted to find out more. Most laughed at him, saying he was stupid. If you owned a big chunk of land with big trees, the thing to do was cut them down, grab the money, and run. But some people looked at what he was doing and said, "This system has potential."

When Merve finished his third cut in 1955, he couldn't keep his success a secret any longer. He had enough statistics by now to know he had the answer to sustainable forestry in British Columbia. He wrote to the minister of forests to come to Wildwood and have a look. He saw his province's forests being destroyed and he was simply not the kind of man who could sit back and say, "Well, it's no skin off my nose." To Merve that would have been tantamount to condoning the rape of the land.

Merve didn't just care about himself; he cared about the future of his children and his grandchildren and the grandchildren of his friends and neighbours. He grew up with the understanding that he was a member of a community and he was responsible for how that community functioned. So when he realized clear-cutting was not necessary, and he had an alternative system that would work, he said to anyone who would listen—and to some who would not— "Enough already! Those bums are destroying the earth!"

The forestry minister didn't come but he did send his chief forester, Dick Spillsbury. Dick looked over Merve's land and said, "This is a wonderful system." But he also added, "The way Canadians are and the way they love the dollar, it will be difficult to make it fly." The two men became friends for life.

Dick Spillsbury's visit didn't change the way trees were logged in British Columbia. Undeterred, Merve kept writing letters. Eventually his letters were simply ignored, probably tossed into a file labelled "Those Crazy Environmentalists."

Chapter 10

A Late Summer Shower

The break-up of the drama group came at an appropriate time for Merve. He was busier than ever with his regular cuts and his efforts to convert others to his way of thinking.

> *I was not really recognized by anybody. Some said, "Oh, he's a nut —he's crazy." Others said, "Oh well, you'll get tired of that." Others simply refused to have anything to do with me.*
>
> *On the other hand, the sub-contractors I was hiring loved what I was doing. The mills I was supplying—I'd sorted out the good ones by now—were eager to get my timber. Two of them admitted I was smart not to cut it all at once and asked if they could depend on me for having an annual cut.*

A man named Andrew Vanger Sr. owned one of the mills. Merve shipped to him for twenty years. Vanger was an honest man and good to deal with. He and Merve struck up an excellent working relationship and a lasting friendship. In Merve's opinion Vanger knew how to run a mill. He had good help and paid them well. As a result, they stayed with him and became proficient at their jobs. Vanger made money on the efficiency of his mill, not on gouging or cheating individuals who supplied him with lumber. He had seen Merve's operation and knew the quality of wood that was on Merve's land. He also knew that Merve's timber was easily accessible. So whenever Vanger had a special order, he called Merve. If it wasn't too big an order, Merve knew he could supply it by cutting back on his next cut. Special orders came with special prices: double the usual fee.

> *One time he phoned and wanted sixteen pieces of timber, 22 by 22 inches square. Now that would hold up the Empire State Building— and I never thought to ask what those pieces were wanted for! It was one order, 16 feet long and having no more than one knot per piece*

up to about one and a half inches in diameter. Now that order needed special logs. For Andy to have taken that order to the open market, he would have had to buy two or three booms of logs to sort out the pieces he needed.

But because I could cut the trees to suit his order, I cut twelve trees. He bought the logs at twice the going rate plus a 10 percent bonus and he bought the rest of the tree at the regular price. You couldn't lose on a deal like that."

Merve was beginning to see how the forest industry could be integrated. He knew that his methods were working and he wanted others to follow suit, but he wasn't very successful at getting them to do so.

People didn't know and still don't know anything about forestry or timber. It has deliberately been kept out of the school curriculum, whereas it's in the curriculum of all the schools in Western Europe. Kids there are taught the basics of forestry from the time they're in kindergarten. They can't be fooled. But here people don't know what it's all about. They have no idea what a unit of wood is. They don't know what a fair price is, and they don't know anything about scaling or grading and it's because they've been kept ignorant.

So I come along and tell a man that he can make a cut every year or two years or five years, and he can spread his income over a period of time, and just as he's convinced, someone will slip in and say, "I'll give you so much cash for it." Well, it sounds big, but the guy who makes that offer invariably has cruised the timber without you knowing it. He's been in and had a look at it or he's had somebody do it for him. He knows the volume that's in there and you don't, so he makes you a cash offer and he doubles his money or more than doubles it.

Cash offers were and still are a common occurrence. On his third cut, Merve had to bring in a new man to do the yarding—hauling the logs out of the forest prior to transporting them to the mill. The man he'd used previously had put his back out. So Stuart Chadwick came along to yard Merve's logs.

When the cut and all of the work were finished, Merve asked, "How much do I owe you?"

"I've got a proposition for you," Stuart replied. "I've got 100 acres of timber I've contracted to yard out. How about coming in and doing the falling for me? We won't worry now about my payment for this. When you've finished falling, we'll see who owes who what. How does that sound?"

"That sounds good," Merve said.

"Fine then. I'll take you up and show you."

Merve and Stuart went up to look at the land. It was near Coombs, a small village on the road to Port Alberni and the west coast of Vancouver Island. The man who owned it had always dreamed of farming, and this land was his dream come true. Merve had never been in favour of clear-cutting, but here was a case where he could see the point. Though the land was densely wooded, it was rich and arable and would make an excellent farm.

Merve assessed the quality and amount of timber on the land. The farther he went into the stand, the better the soil and the bigger the timber. The trees in the centre were more than twice the size of the others.

The timber had already been sold, so the land was ready for clearing. Merve started falling the trees early on a Monday morning. He was taking a coffee break at about 10 a.m. when the owner of the land came and introduced himself.

"You're the faller," he said. "I talked to Stuart on the weekend and he said you'd be here this morning. I thought I'd stop by and say hi and see how you're doing."

"It's going well," Merve said. "This is a very easy place to fall. It's a shame to clear it all out, but if you want to farm, this is good land for it and this should do it."

"Yes," the other man said. " I've always wanted to do this and selling off this timber will help me get into it. I guess I did pretty good. I got $1,500 for it."

Merve dropped the mug of coffee he had just raised to his mouth. "What! Fifteen hundred dollars?"

"Yes. Do you think that's fair?"

"Look," Merve said. "Just from where I'm sitting I can see $1,500 worth and I can only see a quarter of the way down your property. Have you signed anything?"

"The buyer is supposed to be out this afternoon at about 5:30 with the papers to sign," the man replied.

"I walked through this with Stuart the other day," Merve said. "If you'll give me until 10 a.m. tomorrow, I'll bring you a certified cheque for $4,500."

"You're kidding!"

"No, I'm not. If you haven't signed anything, tell the man you won't. I can be here with a certified cheque tomorrow morning."

"You've got to be kidding!"

"No, I'm not."

Merve walked the man through his property. "This is excellent timber," Merve said. "I'll make a couple of hundred dollars on it. See what happens tonight when he comes—and phone me. As far as I'm concerned, as long as you haven't signed anything, the deal is on."

The man phoned at 6:30 that evening.

"How did you make out?" Merve asked.

"Well, he gave me a cheque for $5,500."

"That's right on," Merve said. "I was going to have some expenses and I needed to make a bit—so that's right on."

Those sorts of deals go on all the time. If you go after the people they'll say, "Well, that was our salesman or our buyer." They'll pass the buck like crazy. But the company knows darn well what the buyer's doing.

* * *

It was 1948. On the surface, life was following its daily routine, but underneath the surface something just didn't feel right. Something had changed in Merve and Mary's relationship. There was nothing either one could put their finger on. They were feeling stressed without any specific cause for the stress. Merve wondered whether it was his fault. For her part, Mary wasn't feeling well and wondered whether there was something wrong with her. There were times they looked at each other with the knowledge that what was happening to them wasn't normal. Their relationship had changed. But why?

It was a busy time. Merve was on the board of the credit union, he was helping to get the co-op going, the activity club was going full blast, and Denis was involved in his own share of activities that required one parent or another to chauffeur him around.

They had the garden and the poultry to look after and the housework to do. Merve would occasionally hire some of the boys to help with the garden and the poultry, while Mary would hire some of the girls to help in the house. In return she taught them her considerable cooking and handicraft skills.

Mary's headaches got worse. Her doctor—and he was one of the best in Nanaimo—could find no cause for them. Mary wasn't allergic to any foods and she wasn't under any unusual stress. As the headaches worsened, he gave her stronger sedatives. They worked for a while but the pain always came back with redoubled force.

Mary wasn't the only local resident with unusual headaches. Jim Galloway, Vera Stygar, and Gisele Taylor—all close friends—had come down with these headaches too. Vera and Gisele were diagnosed with brain tumours. Gisele died after an operation that briefly left her with no quality of life whatsoever. Jim Galloway's tumour spread so rapidly that he died before it was even diagnosed. Vera had an operation and was left with little ability to lead any sort of life at all.

Mary's symptoms were the same as those of her friends, and they couldn't help but wonder if they shared some common experience. Like her friends, Mary had been outdoors during a rain shower brought in by the prevailing westerly wind. The late summer shower had occurred three weeks after the Americans dropped the atomic bombs on Hiroshima and Nagasaki.

Before Jim Galloway died, he requested an autopsy. For the sake of his family and his community he wanted the cause of his headaches and death to be known. His massive brain tumour was diagnosed as the type that was commonly triggered by exposure to radiation. The same kind of tumour was detected in a group of Canadian soldiers after they had been exposed to radiation in the Nevada desert.

Merve concluded that the shower that had fallen on Western Canada contained atomic residue, but by the time the Canadian government admitted it was aware that radioactive rain had reached B.C. and Alberta, it was too late for Mary and her friends.

Mary had been gardening on the day of the shower. It was just a typical light rain—not serious enough to bring her indoors—so she kept on with her digging and weeding. Merve was doing some work on a neighbour's house that day. It was an interior finishing job and the rain didn't touch him. Mary and Merve discussed the possibility of a tumour once. Mary warned Merve that she might have one, but he wouldn't hear of it.

When Mary's doctor realized that even the sedatives weren't helping, he began to suspect that the problem might be very serious indeed. He made arrangements for Mary to go to Vancouver for a brain scan. It was the same clinic her friends had gone to. Whether the doctor told her he suspected a tumour is a moot point. The fact that he wanted the test was enough to alert her to the danger. Shortly before Mary was due to go to Vancouver, Merve had to go to the neighbourhood activity club to make a report. Mary begged off, saying she didn't feel well.

My father was aware that I was going and he said he'd pop down and see Mary while I was gone. Denis had gone to bed. He was an early to bed and early to rise guy and he'd zonked right out. He was not aware that his mother had left the house. My dad was just coming into the house when he heard a shot.

He looked to see if my gun was in the usual place and it wasn't. I came home minutes later and he said to me, "I think this is going to be a real sad situation. The gun is missing and I heard a shot.

So we went looking and I found Mary in the woods. She was lying stretched out … the shotgun at her side.

Mary had put the shotgun to her head and pulled the trigger. Merve's world was blown apart.

She knew how to use a weapon, so she had done a very complete and thorough job. She'd left a note behind saying that she just couldn't face up to the idea of an operation that had left her friends as vegetables. She was quite positive in her own mind that she had a brain tumour. And she said "I love you" and "Good-bye" and "Take care of Denis." She was a very calm, collected person and the note was very sweet and very much to the point.

Mary took her life when she was 37 years old.

Shock, tears, guilt—to this day, Merve wonders what might have happened if he had not gone to the meeting that night. What might he have done differently in his life? Was he good enough to her? Was he an understanding husband? Could he have made a difference?

Mary, what did you do this for? And then I knew what she'd done it for. And then I thought I'd made some mistakes. I'm very sorry. I'm so sorry if I did anything to hurt you … but why this? Why did you do this? What if the operation had been successful? All of a sudden, someone I'd lived with for sixteen years was gone. I loved her very, very much.

What do you say about the most excruciating experience of your life? Having Denis to share it with helped a little … but there are no words to describe the pain that went on and on and on.

Denis broke down and wept when Merve told him. He'd been very attached to his mother, so her death had a tremendous effect on him. Although he had two loving grandmothers who did their best to take Mary's place, he missed his mother dearly and his loss of her left a void in his heart.

It was never certain whether Mary actually had a brain tumour. There wasn't enough brain left to do an autopsy. But when the doctor correlated her symptoms with those of others in the area, he had little doubt. And he told Merve that Mary had been a very brave person.

In his report, the coroner stated that Mary was a victim of the sharp increase in brain tumours in Western Canada. She was the third suicide he'd seen that was a direct result of it. "I feel absolutely clear about that," he told Merve.

Merve had suffered a tremendous loss, but the couple had built up a wide circle of friends who rallied around him and did what they could to help. They made all the difference.

Mary had left a 15-year-old son. She had written in her note: "Take care of Denis." It was a responsibility Merve took seriously. He could imagine Mary watching him—maybe looking down at him—and she wouldn't be very happy if he didn't live up to his commitments. Despite his broken heart, Merve's deep, practical streak remained untouched. He hired a woman to come in a couple of days a week to wash laundry, clean house, and help with meal preparation.

There were commitments and activities that kept me from going berserk. There were old customers and people who depended on what I did for them. And so I carried on with my work and I made sure I did a good job. And I felt the loss of someone who had been so close to me that she had almost been a part of me.

Everything changed—every tiny detail of life—from the way he ate breakfast in the morning to the way he went to bed at night.

It was a major adjustment—not necessarily in how I thought or in my ideals—but in a physical way. And then too, for a long while, even though I was assured by friends, and the doctor, and even the coroner that it was really not my fault, I still felt for a long time, is there something I could have done? There was one thing I was annoyed at myself over—for not having jumped up and down sooner and screamed louder for more medical attention to those headaches. I'm not sure that it would have made any difference in the long run. It may have just prolonged it perhaps.

But it did leave me with a complete and thorough disgust for brass hats and the military—the people who go out and create wars to satisfy their egos and their stature in the army. They go out and sell goods to the enemy, to the nation who they know is going to be the enemy. As one officer said when I questioned him about the Nanoose Bay testing range, when I asked what it was all about—after all, the war was over—"Well, we may find an enemy one of these days."

And that's what happens. We knew darn well we were arming the Japanese to attack us. The United States and every other country knew that the Japanese were buying everything they possibly could— to attack what? They weren't going to attack someone who doesn't have wealth. They wanted something they didn't have and America had that. The same thing with Hitler. So I have very little respect for the army and navy people—not as individuals but collectively. I know some very fine fellows who are in the army and they really sincerely think they are doing something worthwhile. I question it.

The military brass—who always manage to stay home while someone else gets killed—I have nothing but disgust for them. This unnecessary event that happened in my life has done nothing to endear them to me. I save my most severe hatred for the armament makers and those who support them.

As time passed, Merve's acute sadness took on a different form. He would never forget Mary, but she and the times they shared together became part of his memories. Among them were memories of friends and times they'd spent with them. It was those friends who helped pull Merve through.

The "Wildwood" sign at the entrance to Merve's forest.

The old hay barn.

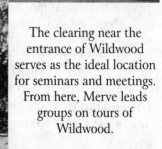

The clearing near the entrance of Wildwood serves as the ideal location for seminars and meetings. From here, Merve leads groups on tours of Wildwood.

Wildwood forest.

Merve has left this section of his forest completely untouched to demonstrate what Vancouver Island looked like when the Europeans first arrived.

A deck of logs waiting to be milled at the mill site on Merve's property.

Wildwood forest.

A horse's head carved in 1999 by a horse logger during a logging demonstration. It took the logger three hours to carve it, using three sizes of chainsaws.

Chapter 11

Politics

Merve's forest also served as a healing place during the time after Mary's death. It wasn't just the beauty and stateliness of the forest giants that healed his soul—it was the physical labour that tired him, satisfied him, and gave him a feeling of place in life.

Until about 1954, Merve worked with a partner. In those days you felled trees using a two-man saw. The first successful one-man saw didn't come on the market until the mid-1950s.

Merve's first partner moved away after five years, and a second chap lasted eighteen months before he sold out to Percy, a friend of Merve. Those were the days when young men did some pretty crazy things out in the woods, and Percy was no exception.

Merve usually took the heavy end of the saw, especially when the trees were on steep slopes. Percy would handle the light end.

One time Merve and Percy were falling a big cedar tree on a side hill. The tree was a cathedral cedar, so called because years earlier it had broken 40 feet up and had formed seven tops like organ pipes. It was all good wood. Some of the tops were two feet in diameter.

They felled the tree, but when it came down, it didn't hit the ground. The huge limbs had hung it up and there was no way of bucking off the first log. Merve climbed up the 40-foot trunk with the saw. He cut down one side halfway through and then started on the other side until he could feel the tree begin to groan. He tossed the saw into the bushes below and skedaddled down to safety before the tree broke off seconds later.

While the main trunk now lay horizontal, the seven massive pipes had been thrust upright again, so Merve and Percy felled each individual top. Cutting the trunk in half, they got nine substantial logs out of the one tree.

Percy had one failing offsetting a great sense of humour—he also had a temper. It could flash and disappear as quickly as it had flared up. One day he was trying to clear out a spiraea bush to get at a tree he wanted to fall. The spiraea kept springing back at him. Percy made three passes with his axe and then really let go with the fourth swing. His axe flew right past the spiraea and through his shoe, slitting the leather from the toe to the instep. He stopped dead and looked down at his foot. He sat down and continued to stare at it.

"Is it sore?" Merve asked, thinking for sure that his foot was split and wondering how to handle the accident with only his small first aid kit.

"No, it's not," Percy said. "It's crazy, but it's not sore."

Merve gently eased Percy's boot off, still convinced he'd find missing toes at the very least. The boot was split, the sock was split, and there was a tiny scratch on Percy's skin.

Merve can still hear Percy's sigh of relief. "Well, I'm not a chain smoker," he said. "But I'm going to smoke a couple of cigarettes right now." And he smoked three before he went back to work.

✷ ✷ ✷

In 1952, Merve was still grieving and angry. An old friend came along to help redirect Merve's energy and take his mind off his grief.

After the breakup of a Liberal-Conservative coalition government, the Liberals, led by Premier Byron Johnson, were expected to win the election. The CCF were nipping at their heels. The CCF were nipping at their heels. Merve's friend Ron Riley had won the CCF nomination for the Cariboo. Riley had grown up in Cedar. When Ron met and married his wife Florence, they decided to homestead up in the Cariboo. Ron's family was from Yorkshire with a mining background similar to Merve's family. Naturally, they had a long history of supporting the Labour government as well.

Ron and Merve, in fact, had developed their friendship as charter members in the Sam Guthrie CCF Club in Cedar. Sam Guthrie had represented Cedar as a Labourite and as an independent for several terms in the legislature. He was considered to be absolutely incorruptible. You couldn't knock Sam Guthrie down; he just bounced back like a rubber ball. Guthrie was highly regarded as an exceptionally fine fellow and most deserving of being commemorated in a new political movement that supported his values.

Ron and Florence were very sorry about Mary's death, so when Ron got the nomination he phoned Merve. "How about coming up and doing the campaign with me and having a bit of a holiday from your regular work? Come and be my campaign manager."

Merve liked public speaking and he loved the limelight. Ron believed there was a need for people to learn about the things Merve was involved in like the credit union and the co-op. He also wanted Merve to spread his views on forestry.

"You could do an awful lot on the campaign trail to help get your ideas over," Ron said.

That was all the convincing Merve needed. He talked it over with Denis, who said he'd be quite happy to stay with his grandmother. So Merve left for a three-week campaign blitz in the Cariboo.

Merve found his first and only foray into campaigning a fascinating experience. Ron's first task was to file his nomination papers in Quesnel, the northern B.C. town that was the heart of the Cariboo. Four men were running and due to file before noon on the appointed day. There was the Liberal, the Conservative, Ron for the CCF, and a man running for the fledgling Social Credit Party.

Ron and the Conservative candidate met and chatted for a while. The Liberal candidate arrived and introduced himself, and the three men fell to talking amiably. By the time the clock was about to strike noon, the Socred candidate had still not arrived.

"I know he's on his way," Ron said to the clerk. "He may have had a flat tire or something like that. I will really, really object if you close this office before this man has a chance to file."

The Liberal candidate laughed. "What does it matter? If he doesn't run, we'll all stand a better chance."

Suppressed chuckles filled the room. But Ron didn't laugh.

"No," he said. "That's not democracy. This man has a right to run and I'm going to raise hell if he doesn't have that opportunity. Give him until 12:30—that's fair. Then the law's the law and you can close."

Ron Riley prevailed, and at 12:22 p.m. the Socred came in with his papers, all out of breath. And was he grateful? Not at all. He was snotty to every candidate there and particularly to Ron.

Merve had little time for bad manners. "Look, buster," he said, "if it hadn't been for the man you're being so antagonistic to, you wouldn't even be in the running. The clerk here was all set to shut at twelve noon. Ron raised hell and had it extended to twelve-thirty. So mind your manners—or get some!"

The Socred man's answer to Merve's lecture was to slam out of the building.

Ron and Merve didn't win the election—that Socred candidate did—but they ran a good campaign.

Merve found people's reactions to the campaign particularly interesting. They were either neutral and posed thoughtful questions or their views were extremely partisan and they wouldn't have anything to do with the other candidates. His speeches were only marginally political. His presentations revolved around sustainable forestry, the credit union, and the co-op.

The campaign trail had its ups and downs, sometimes literally. At one point it took Ron and Merve to Alexis Creek, a town with a population of about fourteen. The road to Alexis was 40 miles of pure mud stew. The car was on a constant fifteen to twenty degree angle to the road either to the left or the right, depending on the unevenness of the ruts. Twice the men had to borrow a fence rail from a nearby field to cover a rut that was too deep. They were meticulous about returning the rail to the fence when they were done with it.

The strangest and undoubtedly the best stop on the campaign trail was in Likely, B.C. The innkeeper of the town was a keen supporter of the CCF and shut down the beer parlour from 7 to 8:30 p.m. because it was the only place in town big enough to hold everybody.

Mike, a fiery Irishman with a keen wit about him, was a staunch Liberal supporter. Little did he know what he was in for when he walked into his favourite beer parlour near 7:00 p.m. that evening.

"Oh, here's Mike! Grab him!" a man yelled as Mike walked in. Before Mike had a chance to assess the situation and make himself scarce, three or four burly fellows had him pinned in a chair.

"You came for a beer and now you're going to listen to somebody else talk for a change," one of them said.

Mike adamantly did not want to sit through a CCF meeting. But the men held him down so he had no choice. The political meeting took on some of the air of a comic opera, but at the same time it provided an open forum.

It was completely informal and they listened to what you had to say —and then you had a town hall meeting afterwards that went on until the innkeeper said, "Look, you guys have got to get out of here. I'll be breaking the law if I don't turn the key in the door. You can continue the meeting outside if you want, but you've got to get out of this beer parlour." But every facet of politics in the community was there. They all knew each other, they all liked each other, and they all had respect for each other. So it became an open forum. Strangely enough, that was one poll we took by 75 percent.

In those days, the CCF passed the hat for donations at political meetings. The party received no money from industry. The money collected almost always paid for the campaign expenses. Even people who didn't support the CCF would often toss money into the hat. When it came time to pass the hat at Likely, somebody in the crowd shouted, "Pass Mike's hat!"

Mike nearly exploded. "I'm forced to sit and listen to the CCF campaign pitch ... I don't need someone to take my hat and pass it. That's too much!"

But Mike didn't stand a chance against the crowd. They took his hat and passed it around. The crowd roared its approval and later walked home, doubled over in laughter—all except Mike, of course.

We didn't get his vote, needless to say. But it was the kind of election meeting that I think there should be a lot more of. The discussions and the points that people brought up ... "Well, what do we want our politicians to do for us?" "Well, that's exactly what we want to know," Ron countered. "This is great—tell us what you want me to do if I get elected." Ron got a lot of information about what the Likely area needed.

Quesnel was the hub of the Cariboo riding. When Ron and Merve took their campaign to Quesnel, Harold Winch, the leader of the provincial CCF, joined them.

He was a superb individual in so many ways. He was mannerly, he was articulate, he knew what he wanted to do and he wouldn't back off. He had the characteristics of an excellent leader.

Harold had booked a room for himself at Quesnel's premier hotel, the Cariboo Arms, not because it was the best hotel in town but because the owner was a close personal friend. He'd made arrangements for Ron and Merve to come to his room as soon as they arrived in town. When the men arrived, a very dignified gentleman greeted them. "Hello, Mr. Riley," he said. "You're part of the CCF group. I've seen your posters. I would like you to be my guests here. I have long admired what the CCF is doing."

Ron and Merve accepted gratefully. From Harold Winch, they discovered this gentleman was the brother of King Gustav V of Sweden. In Quesnel he went under a pseudonym.

Explaining his generosity to Merve he said, "In Sweden, where I come from, I was a supporter of the Social Democratic Party."

The next day a very large campaign contribution arrived at the hotel in a special delivery letter addressed to Harold Winch. Inside was a cheque for $12,000 from the B.C. Brewers. Much later, it came to light that the B.C. Brewers had contributed $50,000 to the campaign that year: $20,000 to the Liberals, $15,000 to the Conservatives, $12,000 to the CCF, and $3,000 to W.A.C. Bennett's Socreds. They were gambling men and hedged their bets accordingly.

At the time, Winch didn't know about the other contributions but he was in a quandary nonetheless. He called a council of war that included his Swedish friend.

"Look at what came in the mail," he said. "This is too much. This comes with strings. We have our election committee here and I'm talking about you—not the people in Vancouver. I'll run it by them on the phone later. The cheque was delivered to me personally although it's made out to our campaign. I'm recommending that it be returned."

Winch's people supported him. He returned the cheque with a note saying he appreciated the generosity but a donation of that size was unacceptable because it carried with it the implication of possible favouritism. If they wished to write a cheque for $1,000 or $2,000, which was in line with what other businesses were sending, they'd be happy to accept. The letter went unanswered.

I'm afraid the present NDP has sunk a long way. They don't have the principles the CCF had. And that came about by embracing labour too closely and getting tied up with the legal associations, various business groups, and corrupt union executives with all the attributes of professional bureaucrats. These power groups are on the buy. Once they give you the support, they expect results—results not always morally acceptable.

The CCF lost the election but they couldn't call it a failure—not by a long shot. They lost by just two seats and won the majority of the popular vote. Ron Riley got more votes than a radical ever had in the conservative riding of the Cariboo.

It was the closest Merve ever got to being involved in politics, but it sparked a lifelong desire for putting truth and honesty in government. He began to follow politics closely. Merve and many others credited the new "single transferable ballot" legislation with the CCF loss. A single transferable ballot gave each voter a first and second choice. W.A.C. Bennett, the new leader of the Socred party and former coalition backbencher, had introduced the transferable ballot, which became law in 1951 but had a very short life. Given the animosity among the established parties Bennett was confident that many voters would go for the Social Credit Party as a second choice, which is exactly what happened. After Bennett won re-election as premier of the province a year later, he promptly abolished the single transferable ballot system.

Around the time the B.C. Social Credit Party was being formed, Merve learned a lesson that stayed with him for life. Merve's good friend George Wyndlow had been a cabinet minister in William Aberhardt's Socred government in Alberta. When Aberhardt formed the Social Credit Party, he insisted that they have one plank that spelled out what was and was not ethical in the party and detailed what was expected from cabinet ministers.

George and Merve loved talking politics, so one night George Wyndlow telephoned to invite Merve to attend a meeting in Cedar.

"Merve, they're going to form a new wing of the Social Credit Party. There's a meeting tomorrow night down at the Mossmans'. Would you be interested in going along with me?"

At the meeting, it became apparent to Merve that the man the party had hired was a hotshot organizer. He handled the meeting well but avoided all references to ethics.

George Wyndlow quickly tangled with the organizer on the absence of an ethics policy. "Look," George said. "I was a founder of this party in Alberta and we had it hammered into our platform on the first convention, a very good and worthy plank that kept our government from getting itself into trouble. Why is it missing here? In fact, I find a number of programs missing here that were the best part of the party."

The argument got heated. The organizer ended it by saying, "It is our intention to get into power by whatever means at our disposal!"

George came right back at him. "That's not democracy—that's suggesting a rifle if necessary. Just where do you stand? Do you or do you not believe in democracy?"

Yes, he did believe in democracy, he said.

"Well what kind of democracy?" George asked. "Democracy that is democracy or democracy that's only a label?"

"We're going to get elected by any means at our disposal!"

"That's all I need to know," George said. "I won't be joining this party and furthermore, I'm not going to stay and take part in the rest of this meeting. If a meeting of this type is forming a new political party, I have very little hope for the future of that party. Down the road, it will be just as corrupt as anything we've had before."

Merve left with his friend, as did at least half the people there. They did form a new wing of the Socred party that night, although no member of that party ever got elected in the riding.

That incident stood me in very good stead later on when I got active working in the credit unions and the co-operatives. You were looking for ethics. You were looking for things that would work, that were practical, sensible, honest, and decent. That was quite an important evening for me. It taught me a lesson that you had to watch for paid people and paid executives. When they're paid, they cease to be democratic or constructive.

You have to have paid executives for certain things, but the rules must be laid out for them. You don't have them making the rules.

Chapter 12

An Ocean Voyage and a Prediction

Merve didn't return home from the campaign in the Cariboo happy, but the healing process had begun. He had come to realize it was going to take time and that sorrow is as much a part of life as great happiness. He worked hard in his forest and made sure that his son got through his education.

As Merve's healing progressed, and perhaps as part of that process, Merve was attracted to Grace Richard, one of the young girls who had worked for Mary. Grace had become so familiar around the house that she was in and out of it like family. She continued helping with household chores after Mary's death, and Merve was grateful for her presence. She was slim with dark eyes and a ready smile that turned many men's heads, including Merve's.

Although Merve found himself drawn to the beautiful young girl, he didn't at first allow the relationship to progress past the friendship stage. Age was one deterrent. Grace was only eighteen months older than his son. But Merve was lonely; more and more he found himself anticipating Grace's visits and their social encounters. When Grace went to Europe to visit her family, she and Merve began a regular correspondence. Grace had a particular knack for picking out the interesting and amusing details of life around her and putting them on paper. After Grace took work as an au pair for an English couple, the letters flew back and forth at least twice a month and then once a week. It was through their correspondence that their relationship really began to deepen. Merve began to send presents. Nylons were at the top of the list because they were impossible to get in Europe after the war.

In due time Merve made plans to go to Europe. Ostensibly he was taking a much-deserved holiday. In fact, he wanted to see if there really was a spark between Grace and him and if the spark was strong enough to ignite.

Merve had always wanted to take a long ocean voyage, and at age 40 he saw no reason to deny himself the experience. At that time the Holland America Line ran a passenger freight service between North America and Amsterdam. The five freight ships were designed with nicely appointed cabins and an abundance of deck space. He called the Holland America agent in Vancouver, and after a brief discussion and a visit to his office, bought a round trip ticket on the *Dongedyke*, the flagship of Holland America Line's passenger freightliners. With shrewd pragmatism he also put down a ten-dollar deposit on a double stateroom for the return journey in case Grace was willing to join him.

Merve left Vancouver on August 23, 1953. The five-week trip from Vancouver to Amsterdam was like a detour on Merve's road in life. Many of the passengers on the first stage of the journey were natives of California. They had driven up to B.C. and were now shipping themselves and their vehicles back home on the *Dongedyke*.

Merve made new friends as easily onboard ship as he did at home. Bill McDonald, a young man from Vancouver, became his closest shipboard friend. After spending five days loading cargo and passengers in Los Angeles, the *Dongedyke* departed for Europe with 63 passengers on board: 43 Americans and the rest from New Zealand, Japan, France, and other European countries.

They were a mixed bunch but Captain Van Blockland knit them all together. He devised a system where he had six people to cocktails each evening—and never the same six people. His parties were meticulously planned. The background music made chatting easy and Van Blockland was a superb conversationalist

Among the passengers was a concert pianist, travelling incognito as Mrs. Hortense. She was a spark plug and played the ship's piano every chance she got. There was a retired British diplomat who indulged in one snifter of brandy each evening, making it last all evening long. He explained to Merve and Bill McDonald, "When you are in the diplomatic service, you are there to negotiate with a clear mind. You cannot, in some countries, refuse what is offered. Brandy I can enjoy for hours. In some countries, people indulge. After a little while, you definitely have the advantage."

Also on the passenger list was Babs, a former Ziegfield Follies chorus line girl, and her companion, who soon received the nickname "Jesus Christ" because whenever he saw anything at all that was foreign to him he roared out, "Jesus Christ, look what they got here!"

The trip was also notable for the wildlife they encountered. At that time, the ocean was alive with creatures. There were schools of tuna a hundred acres long and wide. There were sharks everywhere, and sea turtles with terns, seagulls, and albatrosses sitting on their backs, sunning themselves. It gave Merve a look at a vanishing ocean and a glimpse at a melting pot of people living together in happy harmony.

Had he known it at the time, it also gave him a hint at his future. Mrs. Johnston, a passenger from Sausalito, fancied herself a bit of a dab hand at fortune telling. She had a deck of cards, very much like a Tarot deck, and one night she said to Merve, "I'd like to know a bit more about you—what makes you tick and so on. Do you mind if I look at the cards?"

Merve sat down opposite the fortune teller and watched her spread out the cards. First she told Merve about his past, and if he had approached the exercise as a parlour game, he quickly changed his mind. There were things she was telling him she couldn't possibly have known. By the time she started telling Merve about the future, she had his ear.

"You are on your way to Europe to meet a friend," she said. "This is a special friend and there's quite a difference in your ages— something like eighteen or nineteen years. You come from different backgrounds. You are somewhat serious about this and perhaps it would be wise if you were not so serious. Don't take what you almost feel is an obligation too seriously. Play it carefully. I see a person who has a lot of ability and a person who has a lot of the same interests and activities."

Mrs. Johnston accurately listed all the things that Merve and Grace had in common, then she said, "There is one problem. Your friend has never earned her own living. Your friend has always lived with her family. She is a very fine person but there's a bit of instability there. You are very stable. How much her instability will count, I don't know. Why don't you just make this a trip to visit? Go back and think it over and if you decide to go further, take another trip."

I wonder still what might have happened if I had taken her advice …

Chapter 13

Grace

When the *Dongedyke* tied up at Antwerp, a Holland-America agent came on board and offered the passengers continuing on to Rotterdam and London a travel option. Instead of waiting for the boat to unload and re-load its freight, the company offered to bus the remaining passengers to their destination. In the case of the London-bound passengers, the company offered to put them on the bus, transfer them to the ferry from Ostend to Dover, and then on to the train for London.

Merve and several of the friends he'd made on board took Holland-America up on its offer. Merve was especially pleased. Now that he was officially in Europe, he couldn't wait to see Grace.

There was a farewell dinner on board ship that night and he and his fellow passengers headed for Ostend the next morning.

Merve's first glimpse of Europe impressed him deeply. He felt the old history of the continent surround him. He was acutely aware of the people who not only spoke a different language, but even thought and felt differently. Above all, it came home to him that he was travelling back to his own roots—to a society that had endured for centuries.

It was a bright morning in late September when the bus set out for Ostend. The trees in the Belgian countryside were turning colour and the farmers were harvesting their fields. To Merve's eye, so used to the vast uninhabited Canadian wilderness, the villages tumbled by the bus window in a seemingly unbroken line of civilization. But while the lack of uninhabited nature surprised him, Merve also appreciated the sensibility of keeping populations in small villages and towns instead of concentrating it in urban centres. The villages were not only an aesthetic enhancement of the countryside, but they also ensured that Europe's best agricultural land would remain agricultural.

The bus arrived at the Ostend ferry right on schedule. The trip from Ostend to Dover went very quickly.

Here we were. It was a nice morning and we were standing on deck— and there was England coming at us—and the white cliffs of Dover— and they are white. And the only thing I didn't see was the bluebirds.

Merve and his small group of friends from the boat stuck together on the train to London. It was while he was on the train that it hit Merve that he was going home. It wasn't a clear, logical thought; it was an emotion deep in his gut.

Here was the land of my forefathers. I'd read about it and studied it but there was something that happened when I saw it and set foot on its shores that brought a fragment of a poem to my mind:

> *Breathes a man so dull that ne'er unto himself has said*
> *This is my home, my native land.*

That piece came to mind and I felt, "I'm going home." It was a very, very emotional moment when that hit.

In London, Merve was one of the first to step off the train, and the first people he saw were the Cashmans, old friends from Nanaimo. The Cashmans were just getting ready to board.

"Never mind that," they said. "We'll catch the next train."

Merve made the introductions and the Cashmans suggested lunch in a historic old pub just around the corner from the station. The old pub had been chartered by Queen Anne and served as a perfect introduction to London. The group of travellers lunched on big freshly baked buns, hunks of local Cheshire cheese, tankards of Toby's ale, and a big English trifle.

By the time the party broke up, it seemed a bit late to catch the train to Leeds, and now that he'd had a taste of London, Merve wanted to see more. So did his friend Bill McDonald. They checked into a hotel in Piccadilly Circus, got a map from the desk clerk, and set off to see what they could see on an afternoon's walking tour. They'd gone about 30 yards when an elderly gentleman stopped them.

"Excuse me, lads, you're tourists, aren't you?"

Merve and Bill allowed as they were.

"Well where are you from, may I ask?"

"We're both from British Columbia, Canada."

"Welcome to London," the gentleman said and explained to them that he and a dozen or so of his retired cronies had formed a guiding service. For ten shillings, he offered to take them on a two-hour walking tour of the city. Considering the devaluation of the pound, ten shillings was about 25 cents Canadian, so Merve and Bill gladly took the man on.

He introduced himself as Bill Oxley and said he knew London very well indeed. This proved to be entirely true. Bill Oxley's tour took them within sight of the Tower of London and past Westminster Abbey. All the while they walked, Oxley gave them a history lesson on the places and the people who had lived there, ruled there, and died there.

They wandered past the Parliament buildings and past the buildings that housed the ministries. Each ministry bore a plaque with the name of the first minister of that particular ministry. When they came to the building that housed the ministry of labour, the name on the plaque was Ellen Wilkinson, Merve's father's second cousin. Ellen Wilkinson had been the minister of education, with a sub-portfolio of labour, which made her the first minister of labour of any government in the world.

When Merve spotted the plaque, he called his friend over. "Hey Bill, look at this! Here's some of my ancestry. This lady was my father's second cousin and she championed the cause of the coal miners in the 1920s when they were having a really tough time."

Bill Oxley had been listening. "Put it there," he said. "I marched from Wales to London with her. She was every inch a fighter and every inch a lady. She was delightful. She kept us going at times when we felt down."

That Bill Oxley and Merve had found each other in the big city of London was a wonderful stroke of serendipity. When Oxley finished the tour and brought the men back to Piccadilly Circus, he refused to accept his ten shillings payment.

"You're not paying me at all," he said. "I don't charge anybody that was a relation to Ellen Wilkinson."

But Oxley was delighted to accompany the men to the local pub for a pint instead.

Back in their room, Merve placed a call to Yorkshire. Grace answered the phone.

"Where are you?" she asked.

"I'm in London."

"What do you mean you're in London? There's a train runs from there to here, you know!"

Merve was nonplussed. "Well I didn't want to arrive in Leeds at a time when it might be awkward for Arthur or Jean to meet me. Besides, I'm still supposedly a day and a half at sea. Look at the schedule. You're going to see me earlier than you would anyway."

Grace had been in England for almost eight months now, living with Arthur and Jean Dower and looking after their four sons. She was a nanny but also part of the family—so much so that Arthur and Jean Dower were prepared to welcome Merve as a friend of the family and put him up for the time he was in England.

Merve caught the train to Leeds the next morning. Jean Dower met him at the station and drove him to their home in the small nearby town of Ilkley.

It was a happy reunion for Merve and Grace. Merve was duly introduced to the family and fed a hearty dinner of roast beef, Yorkshire pudding, and two kinds of dessert. Later that evening, after the Dowers had gone to bed and they were sitting side by side by the fire, Merve and Grace shyly held hands, unspoken thoughts of the future drifting through their minds.

They took time to get reacquainted. The village of Ilkley provided the ideal setting for a slow and comfortable courtship. Ilkley and the surrounding villages were nestled down in the river valley. All around them rose the wild and empty North Country moor: a huge sponge of decaying vegetation that soaks up all the water the North Country weather delivers.

While the wild moor absorbed water for the island, Merve soaked up Britain's history. Almost every day, when Grace's chores at home were done, the couple would tramp through the heather, scaring up wild grouse, and marvelling at the wildlife. Merve was particularly intrigued with the perfectly preserved Roman road that ran straight as a die from London to Hadrian's Wall, the northern boundary of the old Roman Empire.

Ilkley Moor provided Grace and me with a lot of lovely areas to walk on, to hold hands, to talk about nature, and to stretch our legs.

It also provided them with time to talk about the future and they began seriously to discuss marriage. Living together without the formality of wedding vows was out of the question for both of them. If they were going to make a commitment, it would be sealed in marriage. They approached the question of marriage cautiously and practically. They talked about their friendship and they asked themselves questions that had to be answered. Would their families approve? Did they want children? Where would they live if they did get married? Grace's roots were in Europe. Her family lived in Holland and France. Merve briefly toyed with the idea of moving there. He liked what he'd seen, and moving his forestry operation would not be difficult, but in the end they both agreed that Canada would be best.

Grace thought she wanted to be married in Holland where her family lived, but she had fallen in love with nearby Bolton Abbey and was determined to be married there. They decided to spend six weeks in England, then go to Holland for Sinter Klaas, and then back to England for Christmas. The ship back to Canada was due to leave London on January 6. If they were to marry, it would have to be before that date.

One weekend they got away by themselves to a charming country inn. Only one other couple was staying there and they retired early. Merve and Grace had the common room to themselves. The deep comfortable couch in front of the roaring fire was a romantic setting. Merve told Grace about the double cabin he'd booked for the return journey and then he asked her to marry him.

To his surprise, Grace said no. "Can we wait a bit?" she asked.

Merve was not disconcerted. Where another man might have felt rejected, Merve with his quiet, solid confidence in his own worth took Grace's "no" as a pause, not as the end of the world.

She explained her caution as the product of a difficult and troubled childhood. Grace had been born in Ontario during the Depression. Her parents were immigrants and very poor. There was no welfare in those days. Grace was the third and youngest in the family. When she was four years old, her mother died under the saddest circumstances.

It was Christmastime. A couple of days before Christmas, Grace's mother was wrapping the family's few meagre presents when she stuck herself with a rusty needle. By Christmas Eve, she realized she had blood poisoning. Lou, Grace's father, rushed off to fetch the doctor. The doctor answered the door, listened to Lou's plea, and said, "This is Christmas Eve. I'm not going out." Two days later, on Boxing Day, when the doctor finally arrived, Grace's mother died.

Lou almost went mad with grief. Knowing that his wife could have been saved made his pain almost unbearable, but he struggled on and finally got a job. He was a good worker and a talented silver plater. But he couldn't work and look after three young children. Lou's sister-in-law, Karen, came out from Holland to give him a hand. She was a methodical woman who expected order. Grace's childhood memories of her aunt weren't kind.

Shortly after her mother's death, a train killed Grace's older sister as she was scurrying underneath some railway cars to run and meet her father. Grace took her sister's death very hard.

What made Grace's childhood even more difficult was the hypoglycemia she'd been born with. It had never been diagnosed and there was certainly nothing to be done for it back then. Grace had feverish bouts of activity followed by utter collapse. Along with total exhaustion came a difficult temperament.

Her Aunt Karen eventually went home and an old friend of Lou's came to Canada to be his housekeeper. Unfortunately she didn't cope well with children, especially not a difficult child like Grace. When Grace was eleven, the family moved to British Columbia and bought a small farm where Grace finally achieved a small measure of peace.

Later when she went to live and work for the Dower family, Jean Dower noticed there was something wrong and recommended she go to a doctor in London. Grace made the appointment while Merve was there, and they took the train together to London. While Grace checked into a hospital for two days, Merve stayed close by at a B&B. The doctors diagnosed her hypoglycemia and made some recommendations to ease the physical and psychological effects.

When Grace and Merve flew to Amsterdam, Grace's grandfather, Frans Gerretsen, met them at the airport with even more warmth than Merve had experienced in England. Frans Gerretsen was the big warm patriarch of the family. Aunts, uncles, and cousins filled the house to welcome Merve and Grace.

They came across as very friendly, sincere, and welcoming people. This made it even harder for me to understand why Grace had picked on some of these people and said some rather unnecessarily harsh things about them.

Merve and Grace spent ten days with Grace's family. Merve looked into Dutch forestry methods while he was there. In his estimation they were light years ahead of Canada. Forestry was part of the everyday curriculum in Dutch schools.

Their next stop was Bordeaux where Grace's Aunt Karen now lived with her husband Paul. Paul was a professor and owned a vineyard. Again, Merve and Grace were welcomed with open arms and shown the most extravagant hospitality. Karen's warmth during their stay did much to appease Grace's old childhood misgivings.

It was while they were staying in that ancient chateau that Merve came in contact with his first real ghost. The chateau was an old hunting lodge that belonged to the castle up on the hill. It had walls three feet thick and old arrow slots that had now been plastered over. Merve's room had a very old cradle in one corner.

There were occasions, even with the doors and windows closed, that the cradle rocked. Karen, who had a very sensitive and spiritual nature, could feel the ghost was there.

During their week at the chateau, Merve and Grace toured the countryside on bicycles and entered a world that time seemed to have forgotten. They had an opportunity to visit ancient historical sights and enjoy the local village theatre. Merve was introduced to the subtle and not-so-subtle joys of French wines.

I had always enjoyed a glass of wine, but Canada wasn't a wine nation at the time. One or two glasses were enough. Well, Paul was a vintner and he made eight kinds of wine out of two kinds of grapes, including a wonderful champagne.

The second day we were there he said, "You must come and see my wine cellar and you must taste my wine." Instead of pouring me a little bit in a glass, he poured out half a tumbler. By the time we'd got to the end of the tasting and came up out of the wine cellar, France was a combination of a merry-go-round, Ferris wheel, and roller coaster. The whole of France was going around me in circles. It was the only time I'd really been what you could definitely call drunk. It took two hours and a gallon of black coffee to sober me up.

Now those wines were all really delicious, but after about the fourth one, I really couldn't tell much about why they were different.

Maybe it was the lingering effect of the overdose of wine, but though Merve remembers getting engaged during their stay at the Chateau Bruffaneau, he's not sure of the exact time and location. He remembers that he and Grace were having a chat and she said,

"If you still have that ring and you haven't changed your mind, I'd like to wear it."

Merve was convinced it was the reunion with her relatives that had done it. The reality of their warmth and caring for her had to have erased many of those awful childhood memories—memories that may have been fuelled by imagined wrongs. In Europe, Grace stepped out of her shell and let herself be seen more than ever before.

At the end of the week, Merve and Grace took the train to Basel where another aunt and uncle played host for four days. That brief, four-day glimpse of the country, started a lifelong love affair for Merve. There was little about Switzerland that didn't leave a deep impression on him. It was a country after Merve's own heart. It was utterly clean, it ran like clockwork, and everyone was gainfully employed. Switzerland's beautiful mountaintops were accessible and its government ran in an orderly, democratic fashion. Its people governed with their heads, not their emotions.

Our impression was that this was a beautiful country. It was hospitable in a nice way. The Swiss were happy to serve us but they weren't servile. National pride showed everywhere but we never ran into arrogance. I came away from Switzerland saying, "There's a place I'm going back to."

Back in Holland, Merve and Grace spent time with another set of relatives in a small town near Breda before heading back to Amsterdam for Sinter Klaas and then to England for Christmas and their wedding in Bolton Abbey.

Before the wedding, Merve took up residence in the manse of the Abbey to comply with the local laws that stated both people to be married there had to be residents in the diocese. The rector and his wife had converted the old monks' quarters into guest rooms. Each former cell was a plain yet comfortable bedroom with doors opening onto the long hall that used to lead the monks to the chapel.

The first night of Merve's stay, he found himself chatting with the rector late into the evening. As Merve finally stood up to say good-night, the rector said, "By the way, if you meet the ghost as you go to your room, just step aside and let him go by."

The ghost of Bolton Abbey was the second ghost Merve missed seeing. He would have liked to have seen the old monk. The rector showed him a photo he'd taken of the near-transparent ghost, holding a large book under his arm. The Catholic monk was said to have endured a harsh and painful death at the hands of King Henry VIII's henchmen when he wouldn't reveal the names of the faithful. Legend had it that the old monk had been haunting Bolton Abbey ever since.

The day of the wedding came. Jean Dower was matron of honour and Arthur was Merve's best man while their youngest son acted as ring bearer. Four days later, Merve and Grace sailed for home.

Chapter 14

Return to Wildwood

Merve and Grace shipped out from London on the SS *Dauvendyke*, a sister ship of the *Dongedyke*. The SS *Dauvendyke*, one of the older ships of the line, was not as large or as well appointed as the *Dongedyke* but she was a comfortable old lady with no pretensions.

The *Dauvendyke* cleared port early on the morning of January 6. At the mouth of the Thames, the ship said farewell to her escort of tugs, sailed past the cliffs of Dover and Lands End, and by nightfall England was only a dot on the horizon. The next landfall would be the Caribbean—or so the passengers thought.

Merve and Grace had a cabin next to the captain's stateroom and the radio room. It was comfortable with a double bunk and a sitting area with a small table. Best of all, their door opened right onto the deck.

The trip began uneventfully, but halfway across the Atlantic, in the area between the West Indies and the Azores known as the Sargasso Sea, the SS *Dauvendyke* encountered the tail end of a hurricane. The evening sky darkened dramatically at about 4:30 in the afternoon. The captain had been told that his ship would touch the edge of the storm—no worse—and he warned the passengers accordingly.

The hurricane struck at 8 p.m. Grace and Merve along with the other passengers retreated to their cabins. They could hear the wind howl through the cabin walls. The ship began to roll, and as the hurricane picked up force the roll became a pitch. The captain reduced speed to the bare minimum necessary to maintain steerage. The pitching became so severe that the table in Merve and Grace's cabin did a complete flip from one end of the cabin to the other, landing right side up on its feet again.

The bow alternately heaved clear out of the water then dipped as the stern rose. When the stern lifted, the propeller cleared the water, racing like mad. With the impact of the prop hitting the water again, the entire ship shuddered from stem to stern. It was too big a strain on the old propeller shaft. It hit the water 20 or 30 times, then there was a violent shudder and the screeching sound of a racing turbine. The engineer immediately shut off the main steam line.

Grace had been sleeping right through the chaos. Merve shook her awake. "The ship is in big trouble," he said. "Dress quickly and warmly. We may be getting into boats."

Though Merve had no idea what had happened, he knew something was seriously wrong. While he threw on his warmest clothes, a thought occurred to him. He had learned Morse code while he was in the Rangers, and the radio room was just on the other side of the wall. Merve pressed his ear to the wall.

"What are you doing?" Grace shouted at him.

"Hush," Merve said.

Ear pressed against the wall, he dredged up his memories of Morse code. "Sparks, slow down. I can't read it," Merve thought.

Sparks must have heard his silent plea because he did slow down as he tapped out his message over and over.

"SOS. SS *Dauvendyke*. No immediate danger. No water being taken. Dropped propeller. Power lost. Wind dropping."

A wave of relief washed over Merve along with a silent prayer of thanks to Mr. Marconi for his wonderful invention.

At daybreak, a Norwegian cruise ship and a French tanker steamed close and hove to. They checked to make sure the *Dauvendyke* was safe and had enough supplies. Reassured, the ships set sail and the passengers and crew on the *Dauvendyke* waited for the arrival of the *Swarterzee*, a deep-sea rescue tug out of the Azores.

The tug had left 30 minutes after that first SOS call and arrived at midday. She was 180 feet long and all fuel tank. The weight of the fuel actually put her decks under water. Only the wheelhouse was clear of the ocean's waves. The *Swarterzee* was capable of towing the *Dauvendyke* at a speed of 6 mph in a fair sea.

The tug's captain decided to make for Newport, Virginia. They tossed a six-inch-thick, 600-foot cable on board, and half an hour later the long and very slow trip to America began. It took fourteen days to reach Newport. The passengers, resigned to their fate, amused themselves with games. They ate well, slept well, and to their knowledge ran out of only one ration: fresh grapefruits.

The *Swarterzee* towed the *Dauvendyke* into the naval shipyard at Newport News to a mass of newspaper reporters waiting on the docks. The press had made much of the disaster at sea and was swarming over the docks when the ship arrived. Everyone was there: the *New York Times*, the *Washington Post*, and what seemed to be every newspaper east of the Mississippi. Reporters crowded up the gangplank, eagerly waiting to interview the first passenger down.

That passenger was Mrs. Connolly, an elderly woman from Vancouver who had saved up all her life for a long sea voyage and was now on her way back home.

"Ma'am, what about this horrendous experience?" they asked.

"I wouldn't have missed it for the world," she replied.

The press interviewed every passenger on the ship, and if they were looking for stories of agony and deprivation, they quickly had to revise their headlines. Down to the last child, the passengers had considered their two weeks at sea one of the best vacations of their lives.

Ship repairs took a full week. Holland America put the passengers up at two of the best hotels in town and gave them a choice of continuing with the repaired ship or flying home. Only two passengers finished their trip by air. The rest, including Merve and Grace, opted to hang in with the ship.

It was near the end of March 1954 when Merve and Grace arrived in Vancouver and caught the first ferry back to Nanaimo. Denis was there to greet the newlyweds. He'd rounded up a few good friends and together they drove to the ferry dock to meet Merve and Grace.

Before leaving for Europe, Grace's father and stepmother had warned Merve that on occasion Grace could explode over some trivial cause and be totally unlike herself. Merve had shrugged off the warning but now, for the second time in two weeks, he witnessed one of those explosions.

The first time had occurred on board ship when Merve got involved in a shuffleboard game. The chief steward had organized a tournament to while away the long hours and days. Merve had declined to enter the tournament because he was out of practice and because he wanted to spend his time with Grace. But just before the tournament got under way, he was asked to make up a set for two games. Merve agreed to help out and played a few practice rounds before the tournament.

When the big day dawned, Grace said, "I don't want you to be playing in those games."

"What?" Merve asked.

Grace repeated her request.

"But the arrangements are already made," Merve protested. "I can't very well back out now. Besides, it's only two games—an hour at most."

"You think of that more than you do of me," Grace said.

"No way," Merve said. "You were there when I made the arrangements. Why didn't you say then you'd rather I didn't play? I wouldn't have thought anything of it. But they needed a player to make up a set. We're on board ship with a whole lot of people, and out of deference to them I'm not going to pull a trick like this."

Grace was angry. She cooled down quickly—it was over in a flash—but Merve could not figure out what had made her do that. Years later he realized that the imagined threat of being abandoned took her right back to painful childhood memories. At the time, he was nonplussed.

Now they were riding home with Denis and a car full of young people in high spirits who laughed and joked and asked endless questions about the trip. Merve fielded the questions and didn't notice that Grace wasn't joining in the banter. But as soon as they got out of the car, Grace spoke up.

"Things are going to be different around here from now on," she said. "You won't be running in and out as before. The whole picture is going to be different." She went on to say that this was her home now and elaborated on how she was going to run it.

Merve's jaw dropped. Denis and his friends shuffled around awkwardly.

When she was done, Merve said, "Grace, you are being a very unappreciative person. Smarten up. This is bad manners and it's time you learned to mend them."

As quickly as Grace's temper had flashed up, it cooled back down again and was gone.

What a way to arrive home. Instead of carrying the bride over the doorstep, I felt almost like booting her back out. But looking back, I wish we had known then about the way hypoglycemia affects behaviour. I wish we had known how suppressing feelings from childhood affects behaviour. Grace's intense grief over the loss of her mother and sister must have had an influence.

The following day, friends and neighbours came to visit. Grace was cool and taciturn. Her words and actions spoke of disapproval, not welcome. But two days later, when she had recovered from the weariness of travelling, her happy disposition returned. Merve chalked both incidents up to too much too soon and let it pass.

He turned his thoughts to the future. The trip had used up most of his savings, and he didn't trust Grace with money. In many ways he thought of her as a child. For her part, Grace was not naturally frugal. Merve was.

He went to the bank, opened another account, and transferred some money out of the chequing account. As Merve had suspected, Grace ran through the money in the chequing account pretty quickly. She panicked until Merve let her know there was more in reserve. The scare he gave her was his practical method of teaching her to budget.

Merve's cousin Laura offered Grace a job. Laura had been a grade school teacher. After suffering a stroke she turned her house in Nanaimo into a kindergarten, but she needed an assistant to run the small school. When she heard that Grace had looked after four boys in England during her trip abroad, she asked her to help with the playtime activities.

Merve bought a car for Grace and she drove in to Nanaimo four days a week to work with Laura. Shortly after starting her job, Grace's attention was caught by a young boy named Michael who had been shuffled from foster home to foster home and finally landed in a pretty good one. His foster parents were sending him to kindergarten using their own money, but they could only afford to send him one day a week so Laura sponsored him for a second day. Michael was sweet but very disturbed.

He had been in so many foster homes because of the crazy system. They were forever trying to put the children back with their parents. First they would take the kids out of their home; they'd put them in a foster home and break the family up. If there were three siblings, they'd all go into different foster homes.

So they'd be thrown into a strange environment for a month and then the social worker would decide it was okay to send them home. So they'd take them back home again. Well, all the things the parents had promised to do in order to get the kids back would evaporate within a week, and the kids were back being thrown around and abused again.

So the social worker would have to take them away again, and instead of going back to the same people so they would have a bit of continuity, they'd find a new foster home.

Grace became fond of Michael and began bringing him home to visit. Merve grew to care for the little boy as Grace did, and after a year of visits that often included overnight stays, they arranged to foster him permanently.

Michael liked animals and fishing and the outdoors and trailed after Merve wherever he went. The social worker was impressed with Michael's progress and attributed his sudden blossoming to the stable home atmosphere at Wildwood. She could see that Merve and Grace really liked children and came to them with a proposition. She frequently had babies in her care who were about to be adopted but needed a temporary home for up to five days while the adoptive parents made the trip to pick the babies up. She needed a loving home for them, but one where the couple would not become too attached to the babies while they were there.

Merve agreed to the arrangement without a second thought. He had always liked babies and children and he enjoyed having them around the place. Grace also agreed to the plan, and soon babies started joining the household from time to time.

Meanwhile, Merve was setting up for his third major cut. He'd already begun scouting and assessing the trees on his land.

This forestry is a long-term project. It's not just selling a bunch of trees and cashing a cheque. You're looking down the road ... you're planning for the forest so that you have that continuity of income. You're also watching for buyers who are honest because all the way through B.C.'s history of forestry there have been a priceless number of crooks in the game—many of them log buyers.

You can buy from people who are ignorant of what they are selling and give them a low price. Then you can convert that into five or six times the value by simply re-scaling and re-grading the logs and sorting them and sending them to different sources. The log buyers have really skimmed off the cream of the crop. The dollars that should have gone into the pockets of the producers ended up with the buyers.

Grace was new to the business and resented the time it took to get ready for the cut, to make the cut, and finally to put the cheque in the bank. The good news about the impending 1955-56 cut was the healthy market for good logs. Merve was working outside one day when a log buyer he'd dealt with previously drove up into the yard. Merve knew Andy Cowan as a nice fellow and an honest buyer.

"I kind of figured this might be the time you'd be ready to make another cut," Andy said by way of greeting. "I can give you a good price for your product."

Merve invited him in for coffee and introduced him to Grace. While she put the coffee on, the men made small talk and then Andy got down to business. "The price of timber is high," he said. "You've got excellent timber and we'd like to buy the whole lot. He reached into his briefcase, pulled out a cheque for $56,000, and laid it on the table.

Merve flashed back to the day in 1939 when another man had offered him $1,500 for all his timber. Merve picked up the cheque. Grace came over and looked at it. Her eyes widened.

Merve handed the

This heavily leaning tree has widened a crack in the rock it grows in by sixteen inches in the last 60 years. The top of the tree has increased its lean by ten feet. Inevitably this tree will fall into the lake and take the whole top of the ridge with it. It could topple any day, but Merve allows the tree to stay because it is a favourite perch for eagles and ospreys.

cheque back. "Andy, I appreciate your offer," he said. "I know it's bona fide and you're right in line. It's a good price. But I have my own way of cutting, so no thanks."

Andy nodded. "Well, you know our intentions are good—but you're one smart man. So, how about us buying what you do cut?"

MERVE'S FIRST STUDENT

The first person to come to Wildwood specifically to learn about Merve's sustainable forestry practices was Bert Herridge. Herridge, who was later to become the NDP MLA for Trail, was one of three brothers who were horse loggers in the Kootenays. Herridge had heard about Wildwood in the way that people hear about things that are new and different—through the logging grapevine. Merve welcomed him gladly.

Merve learned as much from Dick as Dick learned from Merve. Dick taught Merve about the advantage of making regular cuts at short intervals. Dick advised to cut yearly rather than every five years. A yearly cut has the advantage of providing a regular income and giving the forest a greater continuity of growth, he said. Dick had also noticed that regular cuts produced a better quality of timber; the new wood was invariably superior.

Merve didn't start cutting annually until 1980, and he discovered what Dick had said was true. He would have liked to start earlier, but he had no access to a smaller sawmill until then. The large mills simply would have refused the smaller volume of logs.

Of an original group of four, only two trees are left standing. Two stumps show where Merve thinned the other two in the group because they were too crowded together. One was taken out in 1985, and the most recent of the group was felled in 1998. "In this kind of forestry you thin the trees to keep the forest growing and healthy," Merve explains.

"I think you and I can talk on that one," Merve said. "I don't have any problems there."

Grace turned away but not before Merve saw the disappointment in her face.

Word had begun to spread about Wildwood and it was becoming a centre for people who wanted to learn another method of forestry. People came to see what Merve was doing. Most were doubtful. Many called Merve crazy. But many were also curious and willing to look at new methods.

People came from the mainland and from Washington State. It became an everyday occurrence for Merve to get a letter saying that someone would be in the area and asking if they could drop in for a few minutes.

The more serious visitors wanted to know what my systems were. How did I arrive at my growth rate? How did I decide which trees I was going to cut? Why? Why did I put the roads where I put them? Why not put them straight through the middle? Some answers were simple but very effective. You don't put a road through the best piece of timber you have on your property. Sure, it'll help you take the wood out fast, but you're taking land out of growing potential by putting that road where it doesn't need to be. It can be 200 feet further away and not destroy good forest land.

Merve planted seeds in people's minds. He made them think differently. He made them look at their land from a new angle. There were people who were interested in what Merve had to say. There weren't many, but they were there.

While people came to the forest, Merve assessed his stand and took his time with it. It was only his third cut and, in some ways, Merve was still learning. On his first cut he had gone almost 2 percent over what he should have cut to make sure he'd make enough money to pay the bills and keep himself afloat. Merve discovered that first cut paid more than he'd expected. Consequently, on his second cut, Merve dropped down by 5 percent. In the intervening years, the forest had had time to recover. Merve now felt confident that he could make the actual cut the land would allow.

I spent more time on cut number three than I've spent on any cut before or since. I wanted to make sure I got my forest back in balance between what I'd cut and what I should cut, and also to try to make sure I wasn't throwing it out of balance species-wise. I wanted to make sure I was cutting the right proportion of each different species.

Wherever I see forests thrown into unnatural balances, they are almost always a disaster when you see them or they're a disaster in the making ten or fifteen years down the road. Unbalancing nature does not pay. It does not produce and it does not return revenue and it defeats the purpose of the whole operation.

On the number three cut, I spent more time sauntering through the woods with a notebook, tape measure, and ribbon in my hand than I've spent since.

As it turned out, it was time well spent. Earl Froode, Merve's regular yarder, had injured his back and dropped out of work. Merve's new man, Stuart, had three other projects on the go and was in no hurry. He dropped one of his machines off and Merve ordered a logging truck when he needed it.

Merve worked the third cut over a period of four months. He fed his material into the mill slowly but consistently. Andy was pleased about the rate of progress. In fact, the pace worked for everyone. It didn't pull Stuart away from his other work, and Merve didn't feel rushed or pressured.

There was only one bump in the otherwise smooth operation. The bump resulted in the first and only time Merve ever fired a man.

One of Stuart's projects was at the gravel pit. He sent his other driver to yard for Merve. "He's a good man," he told Merve. "He knows how to handle a machine."

It was true—he did know how to handle a machine, but he didn't give a damn about small trees or saplings or anything else that stood in his way. He liked using power and liked to show off. Merve stopped him on the first day.

"Look, I've hired you to yard logs, not to destroy my forest."

"Are you telling me how to drive my machine?"

"Get off it and I'll show you how."

The driver took a bit more care, but after watching him for another hour, Merve judged the damage rate to be too high.

"Stop right now," he said. "I don't want you for the rest of the day, and I don't want you period."

"Are you telling me I'm canned?" the man asked.

"As far as this job is concerned, yes."

The driver took off in a huff. But Stuart, his boss, had no sympathy when he told him about the old S.O.B. who'd fired him.

Merve stands inside the
gate to his forest and
welcomes visitors.

Merve standing in
front of his home.

One-thousand-year-old
trees dwarf their guardian.

The stump of a tree that
was part of Merve's first
cut in 1945. This stump
shows how natural decay
takes place.

A dirt road runs behind the orchard and leads to the lake ridge.

The road winds down through the forest and leads past daffodils and forsythias to the house.

Coming through the trees, the visitor catches a first glimpse of Quennel Lake.

Stuart put the man on the gravel truck and did Merve's yarding himself.

We should not just let people do things because they're able to do that thing. They must also be accountable to the industry, to the resource and to the land that they're working on.

✷ ✷ ✷

Besides becoming a husband and foster parent, and planning his third harvest, one other part of Merve's life changed in 1954.

After Denis graduated from high school he satisfied his love for tinkering with cars by getting a job at a mechanic's shop. He had always shown a real aptitude for mechanics. Merve's car was always running like a dream—unless, as was frequently the case, the entire motor was pulled apart and strewn over the garage floor.

Six months after starting his mechanic's job, Denis got laid off while the shop was expanded. Too impatient to wait for the company to reopen and ready to embark on his own life, Denis and two friends headed east to Saskatchewan for the 1952 harvest. The young men found work in an area of Saskatchewan with a high population of Jehovah's Witnesses. Denis got a job with Al Markowski, a Jehovah's Witness from the Ukraine.

Denis worked with him through the harvest season, and when the harvest was done and his friends headed home, Denis stayed behind. During a critical part of the harvest, Markowski's combine had broken down. Denis had taken one look at it, sent the farmer to town for the part, and stripped down the machine. He had the new part in and the combine up and running again within four hours. When the harvest was done, Markowski asked Denis to stay and put the rest of his equipment in order. Denis liked nothing better than to fool around with machines, especially big ones, so he stayed and put everything into shape.

Meanwhile, another farmer up the road talked to Markowski. "Hey, that young fellow you've got working for you—what kind of job is he doing?"

"Excellent. He's put my machinery in beautiful condition."

"Well, if he doesn't want to go back to B.C. right away, send him over to me."

Denis spent the winter in Saskatchewan, monkey-wrenching his way from farm to farm. He met just about everyone in the neighborhood, including Al Markowski's young niece, Sonja. He converted to the Jehovah's Witness faith and married Sonja within two years. The relationship between Merve and Denis was forever altered.

Sonja is a fine woman and she has been a really good wife to Denis and they have some charming children. But there's a division there because of the religion and my lack of it to some extent. If you're not one of that faith, you don't even exist.

Chapter 15

A New Baby

Michael had settled in nicely in his new home, but Merve and Grace were beginning to recognize that he had some limitations due to the fact he'd sustained brain damage as a child. He'd been beaten and even had his head smashed into a wall on one occasion. The damage showed up in his ability to learn and in some of his attitudes. He learned to do work and do it competently. As he grew older, however, he couldn't resist telling others how a thing ought to be done. When he became a man, he lost a lot of jobs over it.

But Merve and Grace enjoyed him so much they decided to adopt a child. The social worker, Mrs. Cromie, thought that they had done a wonderful job with Michael and began looking for a child for the couple to adopt. She asked if they would be willing to take a child of another nationality. She had East Indian, Japanese, South American, and Aboriginal children who needed homes.

Race didn't matter to them, they said, and within three months Mrs. Cromie called to say, "I have a little Aboriginal girl. She's five months old. Her mother has given her up because her husband is an alcoholic and has left her. She has one other daughter, about three years old. She has to work and can manage to look after the older girl but she cannot afford to look after her baby. She told me that if I could find a good family with a nice home, she'd be very happy if her daughter could be placed there."

Before they drove to Kamloops in B.C.'s Interior where the baby had been temporarily placed with a foster family, Merve consulted one of the local elders.

"We're thinking of adopting," Merve said. "And we're wondering how your people would feel if we adopted an Indian child."

Merve recalls the elder's words: "That would be very good. This is a good home. You live in nature. I would say yes, go right ahead."

Merve had always loved children and babies, but Marquita stole his heart at first sight.

She was a doll. Her foster mother was a charming woman who had got her the cutest little dress, new shoes, and a new hair ribbon; she had her dressed like a doll. When we got to the door, she had the little girl in the window and we could hear the foster mother saying to the child, "Here's your mommy and daddy to get you."

The baby greeted her new parents with a face-splitting smile. They named her Marquita Jean after Jean Dower in England.

In 1959 Grace and Merve bought an old-style cabin cruiser that looked like rats had made a feast of it. But it had a new motor and a sound hull and cost all of $1,000. At that price they didn't mind putting in the work to fix it up. The cabin cruiser became their vacation home. Michael and Marquita fell in love with it.

Marquita had a real gift for catching fish. She wouldn't eat them, but she could catch them. From the time she was old enough to say, "Daddy—fish," she caught fish.

They were on board one evening in Telegraph Harbour on the northeast coast of Vancouver Island. Merve was busy making dinner, and to keep Marquita occupied he had fixed up the smallest rod with a bare hook, thinking she wouldn't catch anything but she'd have fun dangling the hook in the water. He had hardly got back to dinner preparations when he heard Marquita saying, "Daddy. Fish!"

"Yes, you go ahead, sweetheart," Merve said.

A small foot stamped on the floor. "Daddy! Fish!"

Sure enough, Marquita had a fish at the end of her line.

☆ ☆ ☆

In 1960 the price for timber was low. Consequently Merve didn't cut a full amount that year—just enough to relieve the congestion in the forest.

This is what forest management is all about: to keep your forest producing. So I took out enough to relieve the overcrowding situation and clear up one or two trees that the wind had blown down.

In 1962 Merve and Grace went to Europe for a wedding and a double anniversary. Michael was almost ready to leave school and was on a working holiday at a friend's house, so they left him behind and took Marquita with them. Grace's Uncle Frans and his wife were celebrating their own and their family factory's twenty-fifth anniversary. Two days later, their oldest daughter was getting married. The family factory in Switzerland sent plane tickets to every cousin and relative who lived abroad, including Merve and Grace.

The factory employed 40 people, who were treated well and paid well—but more than that, every three months the family took 8 percent of the profit from the business for themselves; the other 92 percent was divided amongst the employees according to their pay scale. In hard times employees weren't laid off, they just worked fewer hours to compensate. The system impressed Merve deeply.

Merve and Grace stopped in England to visit Jean and Arthur Dower. It was near the end of January 1962, and England was in the grips of its worst winter in 60 years. They were due to land at Sheffield, the closest airport to Leeds; high winds forced their plane to turn around and fly to Heathrow. The buses and trains were running but very little else. When they finally got there, snowdrifts in Yorkshire were nine feet high. Businesses were shut down. People were doing only one thing in England: trying to keep warm.

A week and a half later, when Merve, Grace, and Marquita headed back to London to catch a plane to Amsterdam, a slight thaw had set in but the snow was still piled high. Traffic moved through tunnels of snow. The North Sea was covered in ice.

In Holland the winter had also been harsh. But the houses were better sealed. Keeping warm hadn't been as much of a problem for the Dutch. Of course the canals were frozen and everyone skated to work or to the market. The Rhine was also a sheet of ice and so was the Zuiderzee.

Grace's relatives were especially pleased to see Marquita. At eighteen months old, she was a scene-stealer. Just before leaving for Europe, Grace had made a little deerhide jacket for the baby out of a hide that Merve had tanned. Grace had decorated it with beads and applique and had teased out the edges. With her black hair and dark eyes, Marquita was a picture. Her sunny disposition made her all the more endearing.

After a week in Holland, the entire family—aunts, uncles, cousins, nephews, nieces, and assorted in-laws—set out for Switzerland for the wedding and anniversary celebrations. By this time spring was beginning to make itself felt in the foothills of the Alps. Edelweiss was budding in the meadows and the air was warm.

The wedding celebration took place in the ancient Roman town of Murton, near Lucerne, in an old, restored hotel. Merve enjoyed the party, but what stuck in his mind was a conversation he had with the groom at the wedding feast. He was from Lugano, where his family ran a large resort hotel. People with a great deal of money came to the hotel from all over the world.

The young man spoke good English and during the conversation he told Merve that 80 percent of the hotel's business came from labour leaders and what he dubbed "the North American hospital and religious Mafia." They were the best of guests, he said. They always paid their bills, treated the staff with respect, and tipped lavishly. They liked to sit around the lobby, he said, bragging about the suckers back home who had made their expensive holiday possible.

The young man said to Merve, "The America people must be fools to let these guys get away with this."

One other event impressed itself deeply on Merve. In the early 1960s, Europe was experiencing an economic slump. Switzerland had what the government considered the unacceptably high unemployment rate of .75 percent. To correct the situation the government instigated programs to get the economy rolling again. The government estimated there were 285,000 small businesses in the country. There were no monopolies. To encourage sensible and moderate expansion, which in turn would take care of the unemployment rate, the government proposed to build factories to an owner's specifications.

The cost of the building fell squarely on the government's shoulders. The owner was responsible for the equipment and furnishings. The owner also agreed to hire 50 percent of its employees locally and to rent the building back from the government at the cost of the building plus 5 percent interest spread over 99 years. The rate worked out dirt-cheap and it encouraged people to grow their businesses and start new ones. The businesses remained wholly under the owners' control with no meddling from government. Grace's family had taken the government up on the offer and built a branch of the family factory in the little village of Iserable, high up in the Alps in one of Switzerland's French-speaking cantons.

The last leg of the European trip was to Iserable for the opening and celebration of the new family plant. Iserable had a population of about 300. The people lived in houses perched on the cliffs. Streets ran parallel with connecting streets being merely sets of stairs carved into the rock. The entire population turned out to greet the visitors and to celebrate the new factory the family had brought to Iserable. The village children, dressed in their native costumes, sang and danced for the visitors. The meeting room at the town hall had been turned into a banquet room and after a six-course lunch consisting of local specialties, the factory was officially opened. The ceremony was followed by a ten-course celebratory dinner. The tables groaned with food and wine flowed.

After a night spent in the local inn, the family travelled back to Lausanne and their various homes. For Merve and Grace that meant a flight out of Basel to Manchester for a brief farewell visit with Jean and Arthur Dower and then the flight back home to Vancouver.

Merve's second visit to Switzerland had impressed him even more than the first. The Swiss sense of democracy, their care for the environment, their preservation and restoration of ancient buildings, their openness and friendliness—all of these things set Switzerland up as an almost ideal country in his mind.

Chapter 16

The Fire

Grace and Merve got back home from their European holiday in early May. Two days after arriving home, Merve attended a board meeting at the credit union while Grace got ready to entertain her friends with photos of her holiday on the Continent.

As Merve pulled up in front of the credit union building, the treasurer ran out to meet him.

"Merve, your house is on fire. We'll follow you out."

The speedometer on Merve's little Austin showed a top speed of 100 mph. He proved the car could do it. He raced down the road with a sense of dreamlike detachment that quickly gave way to an acutely heightened reality as he thought about Marquita and Grace.

Had they got out safely? He and Grace had talked of the possibility of fire. They'd talked about what to save: the family treasures that could not be replaced. He thought about the fireproof insulation in the roof. It would help keep the house from collapsing quickly. And then his mind sank into confusion as he fought to keep the rising panic out of his throat.

He tore down their long driveway. Long before he got there, he could see the plume of smoke rising above the trees. Then he spotted the orange glow in the sky. The firefighters were there. A second crew was on its way.

A neighbour ran to meet him. "Everybody's out. Grace, Michael, and Marquita are all safe. They're in the orchard."

The mist cleared from Merve's eyes and mind. All his powers of reasoning and logical thought returned in a rush and he started to do what he had to to save his possessions.

Exactly how the fire had started was a mystery. Grace was on the phone with a friend when she heard a crackling. They were used to having squirrels in the attic and they'd just come back so she put the sound down to a particularly active nest. Then she looked out the window and saw smoke. "Oh God, the house is on fire! I've got to go!"

Her friend immediately called the fire department, which had been in the area on a practice session and arrived in record time. The neighbouring volunteer fire crew was on a practice run too. When they heard the sirens, they followed suit. Their main concern was to cool everything down and save what they could. As far as Merve was concerned they did a wonderful job. They saved his tractor in the carport and they kept his fruit trees around the house cool. Every one of them came through unscathed.

Meanwhile, neighbours rallied round and helped get things out of the house. One man spotted a full barrel of water. "Look," he said, "there's some sacks lying around. We can put wet sacks over our heads and if you pass us stuff out of the bedroom window, we can take it."

People do things in times of emergency they could never do otherwise. One man dashed into the house, folded up a bed—springs, mattress, pillows, blankets, and all—and carried it outside. Though he tried the stunt again a few days later, he couldn't begin to duplicate it.

Merve's native practicality served him well that night. He went into the bedroom, scooped up the jewelry and family treasures on the dresser, tossed them into the dresser drawers, and passed the drawers to waiting hands outside. In the living room, he picked up the cabinet that contained the stereo and some 500 records. How he managed to single-handedly lift and carry it, no one knew.

While the rescue operation was going on, curiosity seekers started to arrive. The news had got out to the local radio station and, as in all such disasters, some came just to stare. One of them picked the wrong tragedy to have a look at. He parked his car in the middle of the drive where it passed through a marsh. Minutes later the second fire engine arrived, barely slowing down as it pushed the car into the swamp.

Other rubberneckers wandered to the orchard where Merve and Grace's worldly goods were piling up. Pearl, a no-nonsense neighbour with the well-developed muscles of a hard-working country woman, caught one onlooker trying to fill her pockets with some of the goods and let her have it with a well-aimed two-by-four.

There was tragedy that night but there were moments of triumph too; there were moments of stupidity and some moments that were

The fireplace was all that was left after the old house burned down.

just plain silly. Merve and Grace had an antique brass cachepot in the kitchen that had been in Mary's family for seven generations. It stood on a plant stand Merve had bought at an auction for 50 cents. Someone knocked over the brass pot and saved the plant stand. One man, ignoring a fine collection of rifles and shotguns, grabbed the fridge and heroically carried it to the kitchen door where it stuck. The harder the man tried to get it through, the tighter it jammed until not even the combined efforts of a strong-armed crowd could move it.

In the days that followed the fire, Merve and the fire marshal tried to piece together what had happened. Because there were tall trees near the house, the chimney had long ago developed a downdraft. To combat it, Merve had placed a cap on the chimney that left a ledge, creating a perfect nesting spot for robins. The only explanation for the fire, and the one that went into the fire marshal's report, was that a spark from the fireplace had risen in the chimney and touched off the bird's nest.

Merve was badly underinsured but he wasn't the kind of man to sit and mourn his loss or to feel sorry for himself. He liked solutions and this was just one more problem to solve. Friends rallied around with offers of places to stay. Another friend dropped a travel trailer at the property. Merve hooked it up to his water and electricity and the family had an instant home.

Ten days after the fire, friends and neighbours organized a benefit dance and social for Merve, Grace, and the children. The benefit raised almost $2,000 in cash for the family.

I will never forget the kindness of these people. Sadly, with the influx of industrial, business, and "should-be" city dwellers, this tradition has died out in the last 25 years. That overfed, overpaid, over-greedy group known loosely as the baby boomers share responsibility in part for this. The philosophy of I, myself, and me is a philosophy of human decay.

The first thing Merve did was build a shack. He and a work gang made up of friends and neighbours had it up inside of two days. It was strictly utilitarian but it supplemented the trailer's sleeping quarters and gave shelter while the building of the real house began. The insurance people came through with a cheque within three days.

Then Andy Vanger called from the mill. "Send the logs in you need to cut for your new house. Tell me what the dimensions are and I'll cut them for you at cost."

Marvellous! The foundation was laid to build a new house; everything was in place except for one important basic: Merve and Grace needed a design. They went through every book of designs they could lay their hands on and not one of them contained the house of their dreams. Finally Merve threw up his hands and said, "Grace, why don't you sketch the house you want and I'll draw up the plans myself."

They had chosen a site just a few yards from the old house. It was a more sheltered location and had a better lake view. To take advantage of the location and views, Merve and Grace drew up a plan with walls that angled at 22.5 degrees. Architects told them it couldn't be done with a log house. The words "can't do" were a green light for Merve to go ahead and prove them wrong.

Merve built the house with eleven outside walls and a 22.5-degree angle in the kitchen wing. He did his own blasting under the tutelage of an explosives engineer. It took four months to get organized. Then Merve started cutting trees and getting the logs out. Andy milled them as they were shipped to him.

Eighteen months after Merve's house had burnt down, in December 1963, the new house was ready. Grace, Merve, and the children—three of them now—moved into a house that had partitions up for rooms, a working kitchen, heat, light, and water, and very little else. It was gaunt and unfinished but it was home to them all, including baby Tisha—because while all of this had been going on, another baby had joined the family.

Merve and Grace had put in an application for another baby girl before leaving for Europe. After the fire they called Mrs. Cromie, their social worker, and told her they'd better withdraw the application.

"No, don't do that," she said. "Don't let this stop you. You're doing wonderfully with those children. Any home you build will be a wonderful home for them … and a home isn't all you have to offer. You have warmth and love and affection to give to some little girl who needs it."

So that summer, Merve and Grace adopted Tisha, their second Aboriginal child. Tisha was three months old when they collected her from her foster mother's home. She was another beautiful little doll. She was lying on a quilt with the foster mother's own three children when Merve and Grace entered the room. To Merve's uncritical eye all the children were delightful. They chatted for a while and the woman finally said, "Aren't you going to go and pick up your new daughter?"

"Which one?" Merve asked.

"That one there." The woman pointed to the youngest.

"This one?" Merve asked. He picked her up and held her close and wondered, What have I done to deserve a doll like this?

Here was this beautiful, fragile, and delightful child. Merve knew that if he could have picked any one of a million children, he could not have picked a better one. With Tisha, as with Marquita, it was love at first sight. How right Mrs.

Marquita playing in the foundations of the new house.

Merve with Marquita, his alittle helping girl,
hauling shingles for the roof of the new house.

Cromie had been, he thought. Imagine missing out on this little
doll because of some silly house fire!

Tisha spent her first two months at Wildwood in the trailer and
the shack. When the house was habitable, Merve moved everything
over. The last thing he moved was the kitchen stove. He got it into
the house and hooked it up. Then he tore the shack down. That
night, the first snow of the year fell on Yellow Point.

It took years to finish the house. At 2,300 square feet it was
larger than it really needed to be, but it was always full of people
and it had no mortgage on it.

> When I look at the huge, monstrous, and forbidding homes they
> build today with huge mortgages (and guaranteed dry rot built in
> by regulation), it makes me wonder—what with vanishing resources
> and planned obsolescence—what priceless fools people are. If they're
> building something permanent, that's fine. This house will stand for
> two or three hundred years.

The entire family helped with the house. Grace held boards while
Merve nailed them or she would help him wedge in a tight piece of
gyproc. Marquita hauled shakes in her wagon, six at a time. It was

Merve's home as seen across Quennell Lake.

her project and she kept at it for months. Michael popped in and out. He was becoming more independent, but whenever he was there he helped where he could. It took a total of ten years to fully finish it, including a stone wall with a pond in the entry, a beautiful stone fireplace, and a solarium.

During that time, Merve and Grace sold the boat. They'd visited all the Gulf Islands and the coasts and inlets around them by then and had seen sights that have passed from the face of the West Coast forever. Particularly memorable for Merve was the salmon run in Jervis Inlet.

There used to be salmon runs in all the rivers. Logging and overfishing have taken their toll. Salmon were solid in the river as far as we could see both ways. The fish were bumping the bottom of the dinghy and moving it upriver. They actually moved us upstream with them. The top layer of fish showed their dorsal fins and half of their backs were out of water because there was no room for them to be any deeper. The river level was up over a foot because it was literally dammed by fish. It was eagle and bear heaven and we saw both.

When they sold the boat they bought a camper van on a half-ton Ford truck. The camper gave them access to entirely new

Merve's sense of community saw him helping others. Merve, an expert stonemason, constructs a fireplace for a neighbour.

experiences: Disneyland, Mexico, the prairies, the Cariboo, and inland points on Vancouver Island. In a pinch, the camper could sleep eight, and often it did.

In mid-May 1964, Merve was working at the Yellow Point Lodge when he got a call from Grace at two in the afternoon.

"I have a surprise for you," she said. "I hope you don't mind. We've been asked to take in some foster children."

Rather than feeling trepidation at the news, Merve was curious and intrigued. When he arrived home, the front door was ajar and sitting on the step was a family of four children: sixteen-year-old Jim, twelve-year-old Colleen, nine-year-old Patrick, and five-year-old Carol. Merve saw four bright, happy faces; the children were clean and their clothes, though much patched, were tidy.

The social worker had told Grace the story of the McFadden children. Their mother had died suddenly of a liver disease. Their father was a fisherman who had to go to sea to earn a living. The eldest boy was studying at the University of Victoria. Jim, the second oldest, was trying to keep the family together. They had been raised in a good home. The father loved his children and didn't want to split the family up.

An aerial view of Merve's house on Quennell Lake

He had gone to the social services office to explain his situation and to ask them to look in on the children now and then. When the social worker visited the children, he saw how hard they were struggling to get by. In his estimation it was too much for them, so he told them he would find temporary homes for them just until their father came back. But in the meantime, he needed a foster home for a week or so while he looked around for more permanent accommodation. Based on Mrs. Cromie's glowing reports of the Wilkinson home, he called Grace. "I have this family of four," he said. "They're really, really nice kids. They're very mannerly—a lot of good work's gone into them and I hate to split them up but I'm going to have to. Could they stay with you for a while, just until I find more permanent homes for them?"

Grace told the social worker to bring them along and here they were. The younger ones smiled at Merve unconcernedly from their perch on the stoop, but Jim and Colleen looked apprehensive. What was this man going to say about being saddled with four strangers all at once?

When he approached them, they scrambled to their feet and politely shook his hand in turn.

"Hi, how are you doing?" Merve asked cheerfully.

Jim and Colleen heaved sighs of relief. This man didn't seem like much of an ogre. "Do you mind if we stay with you for a little while?" Jim asked.

"Of course not," Merve said.

Jim told Merve the family's story. Then he said, "Merve, are there any chores I can do?"

Merve put him in charge of the household fuel supply and the feeding of the chickens. Colleen offered to help Grace around the house and the four children made themselves at home. A week after their arrival the social worker paid another visit. He told them he had not yet found other homes for them.

"And I have to admit, I haven't been looking too hard," he said.

"Well, you can stop looking altogether," Merve said. "Just leave the kids here."

For most, taking in a family of four would have been a daunting prospect. For Merve it was a joy. His love of children continued to grow.

The thing that I find fascinating about children is that they do not have a closed mind. You can run all sorts of ideas past them and boot ideas around with them and they tell you very frankly and very honestly exactly what they're thinking. They expect the same from you ... and it's so easy to do. You can talk to them about sex, religion, how they should behave at school, and if you don't turn them off— if you're willing to listen—they are amusing. There's a real sense of amusement in the angles they come up with. They're thinking.

I find that it's far easier to share with children and young people knowledge that you have gained by experience and information about the past. My fascination with young children is that you have a chance to help them decide what they would like to be and how to go about it.

I'm a sucker for kids but I won't put up with bad conduct. I never have. But nine times out of ten, it's from poor parenting.

Chapter 17

Foster Parenting

When the younger children were ready to leave kindergarten, they went to Woodbank Elementary, a brand new school in Cedar. It was closer than the Old North Cedar school and it left the kids with more time to spend on their home projects. They had their own garden plots, bantam hens, ducks, and rabbits. They took their animals and gardens seriously.

Each fall, Merve staged a show-and-tell for the kids. He gave prizes for the biggest pumpkin, the best ear of corn, the largest potato, the best-kept pet, and other categories he made up as the occasion warranted. The best won the top cash prize, but each child won something.

> *The competition was great. They learned to compete co-operatively. They'd be helping each other and working with each other, and at the same time knowing that one of them would eventually be the winner but not knowing who. It was great fun and provided good lessons in dependability and good citizenship.*

As an added bonus the children earned a small income from the sale of their young ducks, bantams, and bunnies.

> *They were learning to earn from the results of their efforts. Too many of our children today are just not getting this. They're in a real fix. They don't know what to do.*

In the fall, whenever Merve felled a cone-bearing tree, he would leave it untouched until the kids had come to pick them. They picked hundreds of cones over the years and made good pocket money from the sales. The kids kept all the profit and Merve liked to tell them that he never charged them for the kerosene it took to take the pitch out of their hair. All three girls had long hair. Marquita's and Tisha's was particularly thick and beautiful.

A day at the beach—Patrick, Marquita, Carol, and Tisha.

Bandanas stayed on only haphazardly in the woods, so Merve went through gallons of kerosene trying to dissolve the pitch in eighteen inches of hair.

When the new school opened, Merve and Grace along with many other parents in the area were eager to get involved. Most schools had a Parent-Teacher Association (PTA), but most of the Woodbank parents weren't interested in a PTA. They considered the organization archaic and worthless because PTA bylaws stated that teachers couldn't belong. The bylaws also forbade discussion of the school curriculum and staff.

The first public meeting at the school filled the gym. At least 200 parents and interested people attended. At that meeting, the Woodbank School parents decided to set a different agenda. They formed a school committee that welcomed teachers to all general meetings and invited them to send a delegate to all executive meetings. All subjects relevant to the school and education were declared open for discussion.

The Woodbank School committee was the first such group in British Columbia and raised many eyebrows at the local school board. Merve considered Woodbank a good school with an excellent staff and curriculum. The parents' committee instituted programs outside the curriculum that supported more involvement with the community. In fact, Woodbank was one of the first schools to take

Merve made sure that, from a young age, Marquita and Tisha enjoyed outdoor life. The winter of 1963 found them firmly ensconced in a cardboard box for a trip around Wildwood. By 1966 Marquita's new love was a pony called Koko.

its students on day trips. On one occasion the committee was successful in removing a teacher who attempted to introduce racial prejudice into the classroom.

At the same time that Merve and Grace immersed themselves in the parents' committee, the social services bureaucracy became a problem. Because they had foster children, Grace and Merve had frequent dealings with the government's social services. Merve thought they handled some things well but too much depended on the individual supervisor in each district. The system had given them a great deal of authority without building in effective avenues for challenging them.

The government gave foster parents about two-thirds the amount of money it took to properly look after a child. Foster parents had to decide whether they would underwrite the foster child for the rest of the amount or give up the idea of taking a foster child. Merve thought it an unrealistic system because there were many potentially good foster parents who couldn't take on the job for lack of funding.

A woman in Victoria, Bernice Packford, did everything she could to change the system. She created a foster parents association that assisted people who were fostering or thinking about fostering by giving them information and advice. The group met regularly to discuss their problems, the problems of their foster children, and the inadequate financing from the government.

165

Bernice helped Merve and Grace with their problem in Nanaimo. In Merve's opinion the Nanaimo ministry of Social Services supervisor was a particularly square peg in a round hole who stuck to the rules no matter what. If your child wanted a bicycle, it had to come out of your own pocket. There was a ten-dollar allowance for bicycles, and even in the 1960s ten dollars wouldn't get you much farther than a few spokes for the front wheel. Marquita and Tisha had bikes but the McFadden children did not. Bikes weren't a luxury item either; they were transportation the kids used every day.

Merve went to the social services office one day to confront the square peg. "I've got three kids that need bicycles," Merve said.

Square peg offered Merve $30.

"That'll help on one," Merve said. "There are two others."

"That's all we're allowed to spend."

Merve put the money in his pocket. "I'll take that. It'll help."

He went to a bicycle store where he knew the owner quite well. "I've got three good kids," Merve told him. "They don't want new bikes. They just want bicycles to get around."

The man showed Merve a few bicycles he had stored in the back room. They were good, serviceable bikes he had taken in on trade. Merve bought three bikes and brought them home with very little money out of pocket.

That incident, among others, convinced Merve to start his own foster parents association. Bernice Packford advised him to find out how many other people were interested, so he ran a small ad in the paper: "Anyone interested in forming a foster parents association, please contact me." He got twenty replies in a day. The parents formed an association covering the area from Parksville to Duncan. The first two or three meetings were taken up by gripes and bitches and people letting off steam built up from years of resentment.

"Here we are, we've taken on these kids and we don't want to give them up, and every time we mention needing anything all we hear is, 'Oh, I'll come and take the kids away,'" was a typical complaint.

The group dug into the supervisor's background and discovered she had a financial interest in a group home. She would put the kids in the group home and leave them there as long as she could before finding a new home for them. The foster parents group used the information and soon got a new supervisor in Nanaimo.

Bernice Packford also suggested the group contact the Duncan social services supervisor because he was a good man and willing to share information. Merve invited him to speak at one of their meetings.

"You will have an uphill battle," he told the parents. "We're all fighting an uphill battle. I am too. But there are things built into the Foster Parents Act that you can use. If you haven't been acquainted with the regulations, it's time you were."

He pointed out that there was money available for things like bicycles; there was money available for special textbooks; there was money available for a lot of things. The trick was in knowing how to access it.

For the foster families, information was power. The next supervisor in Nanaimo was an honest woman who genuinely cared about the children and the parents and developed an excellent relationship with them.

* * *

In 1966 Canadians started preparing for their country's 1967 Centennial celebrations. Most communities, Nanaimo included, worked to create a centennial project that would fall within centennial guidelines and qualify for a sizeable government grant.

Not surprisingly, Merve got involved. If it had to do with community and if it had to do with forward-looking projects, you'd find Merve Wilkinson there. Many suggestions were put forth: a special school, a new swimming pool—but the one that got unanimous support from the people was a museum. Nanaimo didn't really have a museum other than the one run by the Native Sons out of the old Bastion fortress that was open only sporadically.

At the first meeting, 70 people turned up. There were professionals, retailers, housewives, working folk—every group was represented with the notable exception of the city council. Merve and Grace got on the steering committee. They formed a society, then applied for and received the centennial government grant, which covered 75 percent of the cost. Fund-raising efforts took care of the rest.

The local MLA, Dave Stupich, wrote a personal cheque for $500, but the project received little support from the mayor and council. Finally, the committee put Nanaimo's flamboyant Mayor Frank Ney on the spot and got a $50 cheque drawn not from his personal account but from his company account, the Nanaimo Realty Trust Fund.

Contractors and workers in Nanaimo built the museum at cost. It was a community project by and of the community. The museum was due to open in the fall of 1967, but there was one wall that was bare and another opposite that one that displayed only a few artifacts. The problem was presented to Ted Lindberg, the curator of the provincial museum in Victoria, on one of his consultation visits. Lindberg thought about the bare wall for a minute and said, "I'd be delighted to loan you an exhibit of the Group of Seven from our museum. I'll come up and help you arrange the paintings on the wall to give them the best lighting and exposure."

True to his word, Lindberg brought up a magnificent collection of the Group of Seven that completely covered the one wall. For the opposite wall he suggested a local art exhibit. "You have a lot of artists in Nanaimo," he said. "Offer a prize for the best marinescape, the best still life, and so on—about six categories. Invite local artists to display their work. I think it could be a wonderful boost for your museum."

The museum committee put the word out to the arts community, which took up easel and brushes and furiously went to work. The museum wound up with a wonderful display that Lindberg judged shortly before the grand opening.

On opening day, the museum was packed. Mayor Frank Ney arrived late and somewhat intoxicated. In his official opening remarks, he asked which local realtors belonged to the Group of Seven and where they did business. The joke fell flat.

Ted Lindberg, who was standing next to Merve, whispered, "Is that the mayor of Nanaimo?"

Yes," said Merve. "Unfortunately."

★ ★ ★

In 1969 Merve travelled to Europe again with Grace and the four youngest children. They sailed on the cruise ship *Oriana,* and after a brief visit with Jean and Arthur Dower, headed for the Continent.

On this occasion, Merve made a point of thoroughly exploring European forestry methods. He spent a day with a Dutch forester, a day with a French forester, and a day with a Swiss forester.

I learned a lot. I learned first of all that there was something all these foresters had in common. The product coming out of the forest took second place in the order of things. The welfare of the forest came first. They are definitely more concerned with the welfare of the forest and its health and well-being than they are with the product. They believe if you have a healthy forest you'll have a good product.

It makes sense. It's logical. So they're looking at the health of the forest, they're looking at the mixture of species that they need in order to maintain the system and to maintain a healthy balanced forest. There are deciduous trees, conifers, all different varieties, and now they're introducing our alder over there to enrich their soils and build it back to where it used to be. They place their emphasis on quality rather than quantity and they place their emphasis on the number of people they can employ, not how many they can fire and still run an industry. And the employment is not necessarily in the woods. They're asking, "What can we do with this wood after we take it out? How many more men can we get onto the end of this green chain? How many more products should we be manufacturing out of this wood?"

It makes too much sense. European forestry is so sensible, so practical, so rational, and so successful that we don't want it. What came across from all the foresters was that they were striving for the best forest possible—not the biggest yield—and they always referred to it as "my forest" or say, "I want the best possible forest that I can produce. I'll worry about what comes out of it at the time it comes out."

Merve and eleven-year-old Patrick returned to Canada a week before Grace and the girls. Merve had obligations at home and Grace had a family function to attend. Patrick was far more interested in going back with Merve than spending time with a troop of girls, so they went to Schiephol Airport to catch their 5:30 p.m. Canadian Pacific flight to Montreal. They'd planned a brief stopover in Montreal to visit with an old school friend of Merve before going on to Vancouver and home.

Patrick dropped off to sleep minutes after the plane took off. Merve was wide awake. One of the last people to come on board was a tall Swede who poured himself onto the plane as drunk as a skunk. He wasn't a belligerent drunk, just a vocal one. He talked all right—non-stop and at the top of his voice. The stewardess had no luck calming him down. He was happy and he wanted the world to know about it.

In his ramblings, he talked about his hometown of Bella Coola. There was a vacant seat beside him and Merve said to the stewardess, "I know where that man comes from and I know people up there. Do you mind if I go and sit beside him and talk to him?"

"That would be wonderful," she said.

Merve walked down the aisle and took the seat. He shook hands with the man. "Pleased to meet you," Merve said. "Do you know Julius Laaken?"

"Oh yes, I've known Julius for four years!"

"What about Eric Sorensen?"

"Oh yes!"

The man said he was a logger and, sensing Merve's interest, he started to recount every place he'd logged around Bella Coola. By the time he'd cut all the trees up and down the inlet, he fell into a dead sleep. Merve made his way back to his seat. Within minutes the stewardess slipped a tray in front of him. On it was a small bottle of champagne, some Dutch cookies, and a note from the captain: "Thank you for the public service."

When the plane arrived at the Montreal airport the passengers were rumpled, tired, and suffering from jet lag. The last thing they needed was a customs officer who was in the mood to build bureaucratic face. But there was one. Four lines formed and by the time three of them were done, one line—the one Merve and Patrick were in—was still snaking its slow and painful way forward.

The customs officer was doing everything possible to make life difficult for an Israeli delegate to the UN who was passing through on his way to New York. Merve had never had much respect for either uniforms or bureaucracy, and the customs officer's officiousness evaporated the last of that respect.

"Now hold it right there," Merve said to the official. "If you don't smarten up I'm going to phone my MP—and it's the dead of night so he won't like that very much—but I'm going to phone him and raise hell. You're just being ridiculously stupid. The man is going right on through to New York. There's the plane waiting to take him. What's it to Canada?"

It may have been the words Merve used and it may have been the threat to call his MP. More likely it was his sheer self-confidence and sense of righteousness that changed the customs officer's mind about how he should handle the Israeli, or any of the other passengers. The line moved forward smartly after that and was through in no time.

Merve still felt irritated when he and Patrick left the airport building in search of a taxi. It came in handy because Merve was about to have his first encounter with separatism. Neither the taxi dispatcher nor the driver would speak English to him. Merve spoke almost no French. He blew up again, called them every rude name he could think of in Dutch and threw in a few choice Italian words for good measure. The dispatcher and taxi driver started speaking English, and on the drive to his friend's house, Merve made his position clear.

"If I lived in Quebec, I would certainly learn French," he said. "And if you came to B.C., I would expect you to learn English."

Chapter 18

Life Changes

In the years following the European trip, Merve and Grace and the kids put their camper van to good use. They took a trip to Disneyland and splurged on the Disneyland Hotel and everything the Magical Kingdom had to offer.

During the Easter school break of 1972, Merve, Grace, Marquita, Tisha, Patrick, and Carol set off for Mazatlan. They didn't make it quite that far, but that was a bit of serendipity. Sometimes it pays to "take the road less travelled."

They drove as far as the little town of Guaymas on the Gulf of California, when the sweltering heat made driving almost impossible. Merve and Grace stopped to pick up some supplies and asked the merchant if he knew of any nearby campsites. The merchant recommended San Pedro, only five kilometres away.

"Go out there," he said. "There's miles of beach and it's all for you—probably nobody there."

The shingle beach outside the village of San Pedro stretched for miles and was scattered with shiny bits of Mexican jade, onyx, and other beautiful stones. Minutes after they set up camp, a Mexican family arrived with three children about the same age as their own four.

The Mexican family spoke virtually no English, and Merve's family knew no Spanish, but the children started playing soccer on the beach within minutes of meeting. Later in the afternoon, the Mexican father set up lines for the boys, who caught a nice-sized grouper for dinner. The two families camped on the beach for three days. Merve found the Mexican couple charming, friendly, and hospitable.

The same couldn't be said for the American couple who turned up one day. Merve and the Mexican family had taken great care when driving onto the beach to set up camp where the sand lightly covered firm and solid ground. It would have been disastrous to drive farther onto the beach.

The American, a rock dealer from Arizona, drove his truck right out to the ocean's edge where the water had packed the sand.

When Merve noticed what the man was doing he waved at him. "Don't go out there. You'll get stuck!" he shouted.

"Mind your own business!" the American yelled back.

Merve shrugged. Okay, let him get stuck.

The American loaded his truck with rocks. When it was fully loaded up he started the engine and headed back to the road. He didn't go far though. When he hit the loose sand, he sank like a stone. "What do I do now?" he shouted over at Merve.

"Well, you can throw the rocks off to make it lighter."

"Not a chance."

"Well, down the road they've taken out an old culvert and there's some four-foot cedar planking piled for burning. You can go down there and get four of those planks. I'll take a shovel and dig out in front of your wheels. We can move you ahead four feet at a time."

Four feet at a time? No way! The American gunned his motor and cursed a blue streak. The truck sank lower. Reluctantly the man got the planks while Merve shovelled out his wheels. The sun was nearing its zenith and it was hot work, but they moved the truck four feet at a time. They were within two feet of solid ground when the man said, "Okay, I'll get going now."

"Look," Merve cautioned, "take the time to set once again and you'll be out."

"No, dammit," the American said and stepped on the gas. The truck sank down to the housing. "Now what do I do?"

"That's your problem now," Merve said. "I'm having my siesta."

"Wait. Is there a service station?"

"Well," Merve said, "about a mile up the road there's a man working on a caterpillar tractor."

"Will you go up there?" the man asked.

"Yes, I will," Merve said. "But you've been so damn miserable, I want ten bucks. In fact you've been damn disgusting. Ten bucks and I go. No ten bucks and I don't go and you can get yourself out—I don't care how."

The American agreed to the price and Merve drove up the road to where the caterpillar was working. He could see the operator was completely tied up in his job so he drove in to the garage in San Pedro instead. The young man in charge informed Merve that they didn't have a wrecker but the gendarme at the station could phone for a wrecker for him. "Are you stuck?" he asked.

"No, Americanos."

"Oh."

At the police station Merve greeted the officer with "Buenos dias, capitan. There's a truck stuck down on the beach."

The gendarme reached for the phone. "You, senor?"

"No, Americanos."

The gendarme dropped his hand and leaned back in his chair. "Gracias, senor. It's siesta time."

Merve drove back to the beach. "So what's going to happen?" the American asked.

"I got there just at siesta time," Merve said. "You'll have the wrecker here probably by about 2:15. I think the police officer will phone for one as soon as his siesta is over."

By the time two teenaged boys came out with the wrecker at 2:15, the American was pacing up and down, red-faced with impatience. The truck was so badly stuck it would have been easy to damage it, but the boys took great care in pulling it out of the soft sand. When they'd freed him and pulled him up on the road, they asked for a payment of $20 U.S.

"Twenty dollars? To pull me out of here?"

Merve stuck his nose in one last time. "Look," he said, "you wouldn't get that job done for under $50 in Arizona. Come on! Pay the boys and give them an extra ten bucks for having got you out without any damage to your truck. Don't be so goddamned cheap! You've got hundreds of dollars worth of stones you're intending to steal from the Mexicans. Give the boys $30 American."

The American gave the boys $30, started his engine, and left a plume of exhaust as he disappeared down the road.

The only thanks Merve got for his trouble was from the boys in the wrecker, who came over and shook his hand with many "gracias." They didn't speak English but they certainly understood that he had taken their side.

Merve's patchwork family was growing up. Jim, the eldest, was studying welding. Colleen was interested in art and sang in the school choir. Marquita and Tisha were into band and field hockey. Carol was into a dozen things at once, and Patrick spent most of his time with other boys his age in the Yellow Point area.

There were well over a dozen boys from ten to sixteen years

Marquita, age fifteen.

Tisha's school photo—likely Grade Six.

old who had formed a boys club. The catch—and it was quite an agreeable catch—was that father and son had to join together. The boys planned activities while the fathers helped organize and supervise. Only two fathers were needed at each activity, so each father had to put in only one day every eight weeks. It worked very well.

The club did everything from wilderness camping to fossil hunts and tours of the pulp mill. It worked so well that the boys were reluctant to leave when they got too old for it. Patrick was an active member.

When Patrick and Carol had been with Merve and Grace for six years, Eric, their oldest brother came for them. Eric had been studying at the University of Victoria when the younger children were put into foster care, but he had always planned to provide a home for them when he was financially set. When the time came, he asked Merve and Grace if the youngest two could come to live with him. It was with pride and emotion that they watched Patrick and Carol go.

* * *

In 1971 Merve's mother and father celebrated their diamond wedding anniversary. After 60 years they were still very much in love. The celebration took place at their home because Merve felt they were too frail to go out and celebrate at a hall. But he also knew to expect far more guests than his parents' modest home would allow. Two hundred people came to the anniversary party.

Mother and dad had been through rough times and good times but they always had each other. They had a sense of purpose spiced with a lot of good humour. Their ability to collect friends was phenomenal.

Some of their old pals from the orchestra turned up, so William tuned up his fiddle and Christina sat down at the piano. The old tunes may have sounded a bit scratchy, but no one cared.

William had suffered a mild stroke in 1968 but it didn't impair his ability to play music, nor did it harm his long-term memory. It did, however, affect his short-term memory, so Christina was William's memory and guide for current events. William was the memory bank for the past. His recollection of old stories was astoundingly accurate.

Merve had started helping his parents out around the house and garden but only under protest from both of them. They prized their independence and were determined to hang on to it to the end.

William had always been an excellent driver, and as long as his wife was there by his side to direct him he still did well. But one day William decided to get the groceries on his own and he drove all the way to Cumberland to the old store where he had worked decades before. Luckily, the girl at the counter was the granddaughter of the original owners. She recognized William Wilkinson and said, "Oh my, Mr. Wilkinson! How wonderful to see you!"

"Where am I?" William asked.

"You're in Cumberland."

William was so shocked he didn't even stop to buy groceries but turned right around and drove back home. After that Merve suggested William stop driving and turn in his licence. At that time, when an older person gave up his driver's licence voluntarily, the superintendent of motor vehicles wrote a personalized letter congratulating the recipient on his long record of accident-free driving. In time, William took great pride in the letter he received.

But turning in his licence didn't stop his exploits. One day he found another licence he thought he'd lost and he got back behind the wheel. Merve finally sold the car to keep William off the road.

During the 1970s, more and more people were starting to notice the work Merve was doing in his forest. The first people who paid attention were those who worked with Merve and those who bought his products. Merve's skidder crew belonged to a large family that owned 500 acres. They were so impressed by Merve's system they swung their own operation over to selective logging.

The trucker who came in to spell Merve's regular man watched for a while and after taking out three or four loads, said, "I wish more people did this."

So in '72 to '75 we were just beginning to stir up ripples amongst some of the conservation people and the industry itself. I had something that was continuous. We always had this to come back to. A full cut didn't take me a whole year, you do it in a matter of a few weeks and then you've got other work to deal with. The trips we took, we were able to do without compromising our way of life.

Christina still owned a share of Wildwood and took great pleasure in being a landowner. The property was still divided into two legal parcels. Merve had sole title to the 77-acre parcel on which he had built his house and shared the other 70-acre parcel with his mother. Christina had always wanted her share to be passed on to Merve's son, Denis, and she became quite insistent about it. She was determined to see Denis inherit the land before she died, so she made out her share to Denis and suggested to Merve that he do the same with his half of the 70-acre parcel.

This was to be Denis's inheritance. Being Scottish, the idea of an inheritance was a very strong driving influence for mother. She suggested it and I thought it was okay. Afterward, I wished I'd gone a different route.

But it was too late. Denis may have been Merve's son, but his loyalty to the Jehovah's Witnesses took precedence over family ties. Denis felt duty-bound to contribute the inheritance to his church and put the property on the market as soon as it was legally his. Merve was short of cash and couldn't buy it himself. Robin Field, an instructor at Nanaimo's Malaspina College, bought the land for $50,000. Robin knew Merve loved the land and had always agreed with Merve's idea of forest management. He asked Merve to keep on managing the forest. That suited Merve, but the loss of stumpage fees on 70 acres took a sizeable bite out of his income.

Merve was disappointed and angry but he refused to stay bitter. He looked for a way to put a positive spin on the situation and decided that perhaps the loss of 70 acres was an opportunity. If he could manage Robin's property, why not do the same with other people's land? A lot of people in Yellow Point liked the idea of having a man with Merve's knowledge and sensitivity for the environment looking after their property. Merve's income quickly caught up again, but the rift between father and son was irreparable. Christina was also disappointed in Denis but she wouldn't talk about it.

> I was very annoyed. If he didn't want it himself, he could have turned it over to his own son, who did want it at the time, or he could at least have given me the opportunity to buy it back. I told him, "Look, this is virtual treachery. You didn't even give me the opportunity to buy it back."

In late 1976, Christina developed an inoperable cancerous tumour. Merve moved Christina and William to Blytheswood, a retirement home in the area, and felt fortunate to get them a double room. He couldn't imagine one without the other.

Christina welcomed her new idleness and became a great favourite with the staff. William, however, was still an energetic man but his memory was gone. He no longer recognized his wife or his surroundings. He was quite certain he had to get back home because that's where he'd find his beloved Chris, so periodically he'd march off down the road.

Merve had rented out his parents' home, and the tenants got used to having William turn up at odd hours demanding to know what they were doing in his home. Merve picked up William and drove him back to Blytheswood many times. The staff did their best to keep track of William with the unsolicited help of "the Admiral," who was a resident of the nursing home with whom William had struck up a fast friendship. If the Admiral noticed that William was wandering off, he'd reel him back in on the premise that no one was allowed to desert the ship.

Christina died soon after entering Blytheswood. When they buried her, William didn't know he was attending her funeral—at least not on a conscious level. Merve believes that in his heart and soul William must have known she was gone because he followed her just a few months later. Merve scattered their ashes around the property they loved so much and where they had lived their lives together.

They were two absolutely wonderful people who are gone but not forgotten. Dad and Mom had turned me into a self-reliant person. But there was that moment when they were gone—where all of a sudden a really large door in my life closed. And I realized, okay, I'm the patriarch now. I'm the one who is going to pass on the information that my father and mother passed on to me. It's a sad feeling. It's a feeling of hesitation to begin with. I wonder if I really can function on my own. And then suddenly the realization came and I was able to say to myself very calmly, "The job was done well. I know what I should do in life, how I should carry on my affairs and my business, what good ethics and bad ethics are, and I am now in complete control of the ship."

More changes were in store. When Merve married Grace he never dreamed that they would divorce 26 years later. Looking back, however, he was surprised he missed the warning signs. He had forged ahead in ignorant bliss thinking they had a good relationship. They were the envy of many of their friends. Yes, perhaps Grace was more interested in material things than Merve was: for her, there was never enough money. But as the years went by, Merve believed she was coming to see things more his way.

For her part, Grace may have begun to feel restricted by a life that to her seemed narrowly bound up with Merve's rules. At times she felt more like a child than an equal partner in the relationship. While Merve was an adult with strong opinions when he'd married her, Grace was a young woman who was still finding her own way.

There were one or two signals that something was wrong, but to Merve they seemed insignificant. In 1977, one of Merve's friends died of cancer so suddenly that it came as a shock to everyone who knew him. At the time, Merve was busy doing some work around the house.

One evening Grace looked up at Merve and said, "You know, Merve, you just write your friends off when they get ill."

Merve was taken by surprise. "No. That's not true."

"Well you hadn't been to see Rod and he was under treatment."

"But I never expected him to be dead."

"Well, you just write them off."

Merve didn't understand what Grace was getting at or why she had even raised the issue.

Driving was another source of conflict between them. Merve and Grace had always shared driving duties on their trips. Grace was a good driver and each helped the other navigate. The arrangement worked well, especially on some of their long road trips. Then it all changed. On three or four occasions when Grace was in the passenger seat, she gave him advice that might have killed them both.

"Your driving isn't as good as it used to be," she said.

"Well your advice isn't as good as it used to be," Merve replied, and after that he paid no more attention to Grace's driving advice.

When Merve decided to sell his parents' house and thirteen acres, Grace went on what Merve could only call a spending spree. He cut off her money flow and caused more resentment to build up.

At the end of 1978 Merve and Grace celebrated their silver wedding anniversary. They'd had a quiet wedding and Merve wanted a big splurge for their anniversary. True, they had a few problems, but Merve still believed their marriage was essentially happy and successful.

They rented Manana Lodge for the day. The Lodge was perched seaside across from Ladysmith at the southern tip of Yellow Point. Merve and Grace hosted an open house for their friends. The celebration continued into the evening with a dinner for the family and the people who had helped out with the day. Tisha's Dixieland jazz band entertained and Merve recalled the olden days of chivalry by smashing his glass in the fireplace after drinking a toast to his bride. But even in all the merriment, there was a sour note.

Grace's brother, Lutje, was one of the emcees for the occasion. His own marriage was dissolving at the time so that may have been the reason, or maybe it was just his quirky sense of humour, but at one point he said, "This is more like a wake than a wedding."

Grace thought the comment was hilarious. So did Merve. But after Grace repeated the joke over and over to anyone who would listen, he began to dislike it and asked her to stop.

A year later friends from Vancouver came to join the family for the Christmas holiday. Audrey and Richard had four children about the same ages as Marquita and Tisha, so it was a full and happy house. They were thoroughly enjoying their Boxing Day party when Grace suddenly said, "I don't feel well. I feel really, really sick." She was white, cold, and shivery but without any cold or flu symptoms. Alarmed, Merve rushed her to the hospital.

The emergency room was crowded and only one young intern was looking after the cases. The intern took a quick look at Grace and made his diagnosis: too much holiday partying.

"No," said Merve. If uniforms and other symbols of authority couldn't intimidate him, a doctor certainly wasn't about to, especially not a doctor who Merve was sure didn't know what he was talking about. Merve insisted that Grace stay in the hospital until their family doctor could come around to see her.

The intern said flatly that there was no chance of Dr. Bennett showing up on Boxing Day and besides, there were no beds available. He gave Grace some aspirin and asked Merve to take her home. Merve felt he had little choice so he called ahead to Audrey and asked her to warm up Grace's bed so that she would be as comfortable as possible.

Merve got her home and into bed, but within an hour Grace said, "I'm getting worse."

Merve didn't care if it was Boxing Day. He called Dr. Bennett at home. The doctor had just come in from a visit to his son. He listened to Merve's description of Grace's symptoms. "Bring her right back to the hospital," he said. "I'll meet you there."

Dr. Bennett was waiting for them. Nurses wheeled Grace into an examining room and he rushed in after her. When he came out, he said, "Merve, I'm sorry. We've got something really, really serious here. Grace is a very sick girl. I've given her some drugs to carry her through for now, but I'm getting two more doctors in."

Dr. Bennett had diagnosed Grace with erythema, a disease so rare it strikes only one in 300,000 people. In erythema, a person becomes allergic to her own antibodies and the body literally begins to attack itself. He also called in an eye specialist and a skin specialist. For several hours Merve could only stand helplessly in the corridor, watching nurses rushing in and out.

When Dr. Bennett emerged he told Merve that Grace had been clinically dead. The disease had caused abscesses to form at the back of her eyes, but the worst was over, he said. In the morning, her skin would be covered with painful sores but at least the poison would be coming out of the body, not internalizing.

Grace was in the hospital for two weeks before coming home for a long convalescence. She told Merve about the experience—about being outside her body and watching the doctors working on her. She recalled a long black tunnel with a light at the end, and when she reached the light she recognized friends who had died. And the friends said to her, "Go back, you still have work to do."

As Grace got well again, Merve noticed dramatic changes. She turned away from her old friends, saying she wanted to socialize with more sophisticated people. Merve dug his heels in.

From Grace's point of view, Merve wasn't being loyal; he was being stodgy. They bickered more often. Then one day she looked at him and said, "I want a divorce."

Despite their frequent arguments of late, Merve was still taken completely by surprise. "What for?" he asked. "What are your grounds? I haven't been playing around with anybody—you know that darn well, but I won't say the same for you."

Was it truth or anger that made Merve blurt out those words? He had no proof, only suspicions. But he was deeply hurt and at a loss to explain to himself what was going on or what had gone wrong. In his world, the sun and moon were turning properly in their appointed orbits. He and Grace had a wonderful family, a good life, money enough to see to their needs, plenty of friends, and an active social life. He took Grace out to the places she wanted to go. He didn't like her new friends but he was willing to bear them.

Grace wanted a new life. She wanted something Merve couldn't provide. What that something was, she couldn't explain to him. But he was unwilling to throw in the towel right away. "Let's give it three months," he suggested. "If you want to try it on your own for a while, we'll get you a little apartment."

"No," Grace said. "I want to take over this land. I want you to leave."

"No, this was my place long before I met you," Merve said. "And I haven't given you any grounds for divorce. I rather think that you've given me grounds."

Grace finally gave in to Merve's suggestion and moved into an apartment for three months. Merve was hurt and often lonely, but the girls took it well. They didn't take sides and they were kind and supportive to both their parents. Merve knew from previous experience that new activities would keep his mind off his problems so he joined the local canoe club and kept himself busy.

Grace came back after three months, and after another two months of struggling to live together, she left for good. The divorce proceedings didn't get heated or vindictive, but afterwards Merve lost something very precious: the ownership of his land. The final papers were not signed until 1988. Grace, as Merve's business partner, got joint tenancy of the property with the proviso it would go to her in its entirety at the time of his death.

Chapter 19

Wildwood's Message Spreads

The late 1970s and early 1980s still remain a blur in Merve's mind. He felt overwhelmed by the loss of both his parents and the shock of the divorce. At the same time, the children were growing up and striking out on their own.

As soon as they had been old enough to understand, Merve and Grace told Tisha and Marquita that they were adopted and that they were Aboriginal children. Had they wanted to contact their birth mothers, Merve would have gladly supported them but they never did. The girls loved Merve and Grace; they were their parents. In turn, Merve was able to lavish a love on Marquita and Tisha that he could not give to Denis.

They didn't divorce themselves from me like my son did. I had the opportunity to be with them all the way through. And we didn't have this wall between us—just like the Berlin Wall. When you have someone in the family who is a Jehovah's Witness, you have a minor Berlin Wall. You'll talk to each other over the wall, but you'll never break through.

Marquita had a friend who was her constant companion. She and Randy loved to water ski, and when the nationally famous Nanaimo bathtub races got started, they immediately jumped on board, literally and figuratively. Randy designed and built the boats; Marquita raced them. She was a speed demon. In the second year of the races, Marquita romped home with the World Championship.

It was wonderful for those kids. They went all over the place— wherever there was a bathtub race. The kids who were into bathtubbing the first two years were just a wonderful group. You'd find them helping to shine up each other's boats. It was friendly competition. The third year the professionals got in and the amateurs had to mount guard on their boats to keep them from being sabotaged.

183

Carburetors were altered—all sorts of things were done to boats the professionals thought might threaten them. Randy and Marquita quit in disgust.

Tisha graduated from high school and went on to Confederation College in Thunder Bay where she studied travel consulting and environmental consulting. Colleen, their foster sister, became an art teacher and won many awards in her field.

The fact that the children had turned out so successful and happy made the divorce even more puzzling for Merve. He finally decided it was mostly due to a change in Grace's personality after her near-death experience. At least that explanation was good enough for him to move on. And with determination, he did move on. Along with the canoe club, Merve joined a dance club and a jazz club. His solution to loss and heartache was simple: throw yourself into activity, make new friends, go out with old friends, and in this way rebuild your life. He had never been, and wasn't now, one to sit around and feel sorry for himself. And he certainly wasn't about to plunge into a new relationship before he felt solid ground beneath his feet again.

More than anything else, it was the canoe club that set Merve back on an even keel. In 1984, the club went on its first week-long trip through the Broken Islands off Vancouver Island's rugged west coast near the Alberni Inlet. Ray Foucher, a biologist with Nanaimo's Biological Station, led the expedition. Merve enjoyed the trip so much that he came back determined to learn navigation skills. Like everything else Merve put his mind to, he followed through, immersing himself in his navigational studies and emerging with his Junior Navigator's Certificate.

The next year, Merve acted as leader for the group. He took a dozen members of the club to the Bunsby Islands off the northwest coast of Vancouver Island. The trip was memorable for its wonderful weather, aside from the mind-numbing storm on the night after they paddled to Acous. Also there was the discovery of the Aboriginal elders' place.

The most challenging part of the trip involved a four-hour paddle across open water to reach the Bunsby Islands. One member of the group didn't know what he had gotten himself into, and when he realized, he panicked. Looking back on the incident, Merve knew he should have been alerted to the impending problem long before they even got into their canoes.

Paddlers heading home through the Broken Islands.

I should have sensed that I was going to have a hassle. We got to Parksville and Jerry was asking "Where am I? Where am I?" "Well … we're on the Island Highway just south of Parksville." By the time we got to Zeballos, I think he thought he'd been taken off the face of the earth. He was practically panicking.

Jerry was mostly okay until the group spent the night on Acous, one of the small Bunsby Islands, zipped tight inside their tents while a storm raged outside. The winds picked up to 90 mph that night and rain drove down in sheets. In the morning, the sky was clear, the sun was shining, and the birds were shaking themselves dry.

Everyone but Jerry had weathered it well. He came tearing out of his tent at first light, shouting, "We've got to go home, Merve. I can't stand it anymore! I can't spend another night in a tent!"

"There's no way, Jerry," Merve said. "We're not getting off this beach today. Look, you've still got 30-foot waves out there, and there's no way I'm going to take this crew out in 30-foot rollers."

"But I've got to get away from here!"

"Calm down, relax. You're here for the day. The sun is shining. Nobody got hurt."

"But I can't stand another night in a tent!"

"Well, tonight you can take your sleeping bag and go up under the big trees. You won't have to spend the night in a tent."

"But the bears will get me."

Merve had run to the end of his patience. "Jerry, no self-respecting bear is going to come anywhere near you."

The small joke was lost on Jerry, who was still shaking.

"Okay, Jerry, I'll give you an option," Merve said. "You put on your life jacket and start swimming back to Kyuquot and we'll pick you up on the return trip."

Some of the other paddlers calmed Jerry, and he stayed one more night. The next morning he dragged his partner into their canoe and they set off alone back across the channel.

Merve and his paddling partner, Joanna, also set off alone that day, but they were interested in exploring a small neighbouring island. They paddled across a narrow channel and walked around the perimeter of the island. Soon they noticed a pathway leading to the centre. Merve thought that quite unusual because they were in the heart of the temperate rain forest, where the undergrowth of salal, salmonberry, and laurel rises 30 feet into the air, making the woods almost impenetrable.

They continued past the path, but when they reached the opposite side of the island, there was the mysterious path again. Merve was now so intrigued he wanted to see where it led.

"Come on," he said to Joanna. "Let's go follow the trail and see where it leads us."

Joanna was curious too, so they followed the trail until they reached a clearing that was perfectly square, as though it had been measured and cut with precision tools. In the middle of the 50-foot square was a mossy mound that looked like a burial site. They stopped and stood very still. They felt something: a strong sense of peace or holiness.

Suddenly I felt that we were not alone ... that there were a whole lot of people there. But they were all friendly, and it felt like they were all sitting still and contemplating. It was a funny feeling and there was a prickly sensation. And then I thought, no, why should it be prickly? This is a friendly situation. Whatever this is—whatever this feeling is—it's not going to hurt us.

Merve and Joanna walked into the clearing with the reverence of entering a cathedral. They found a log at the edge of the clearing and sat down, absorbing the peace. Merve's attention turned to the grassy mound. After some minutes of sitting quietly he walked toward it and gently parted the moss. Underneath it was a mass of small rocks.

Marquita, age 21, feeding one of the Wildwood lambs.

They left the clearing as silently as they had entered it. Later, back at the campsite, they told the others about their experience.

"I've never felt so calm within myself," Joanna said. "I felt absolutely at ease. I was thinking thoughts I haven't thought for years: Who am I? What am I doing? Why am I here?"

Merve said he had felt exactly the same way.

When they got back to Kyuquot, Merve found the answer to the puzzle. One of the elders in the native village told Merve and Joanna that that place was where the shaman and the chiefs spent their time when they went into seclusion.

And she was fascinated that I had the reaction that I did. The place hadn't been used for quite a while. When an Aboriginal chieftain or shaman goes to a sacred place, they take a rock with them as a symbol of the most enduring thing they know—in other words, "Our faith is enduring." And they leave the rock behind to keep the place safe from danger and harm until they meet again.

✷ ✷ ✷

By 1986, Merve's life was full again. He had many many friends and acquaintances who dropped in at all hours. He had a full slate of dance partners. He was involved in the co-op once again. He became the trip planner for the canoe club. His forest was doing well, and the men he had met in Europe had started to come to see his operation. He walked the land with foresters from Germany, Holland, Switzerland, and France. They gave him the benefit of their two- and three-hundred-year history of sustainable forestry, and they projected the future of Merve's land and gave him a hint of what was to come. Merve sucked up their knowledge like a thirsty sponge.

Whether he knew it or not, Merve was ready for the avalanche of media publicity that followed him when he tuned in to Cam Cathcart's *Pacific Report* on CBC and shot off his letter to Cathcart. Within two weeks, camera crews swarmed over his property, and after the show aired, he became one of the most in-demand foresters on the Pacific coast. That *Pacific Report* program began an era of almost feverish activity. Merve was in his mid-70s, a time when most men are slowing down, but his pace was beginning to pick up.

> *What I had been working on in my forestry up to that point with the advice of foreign foresters and my own training and experience was beginning to really, really show. I was feeling very confident. I had increased the quality of my wood production, improved the techniques, and improved the way I handled and managed the debris in the forest. I made a whole lot of fairly radical changes in my concepts, all based on the same old tried-and-true principle of harvesting what you grow.*

Soon after the program aired, Merve was asked to speak at the horse loggers convention in Quesnel, B.C. Merve said yes and continued to say yes to any opportunity to promote sustainable forestry. About 120 horse loggers had come to the convention to swap ideas and techniques and to compare notes.

Shortly after that first convention, Merve received an invitation from the Canadian Restoration and Environmental Development Association (CREDA) in McBride, a tiny community near the northern B.C.-Alberta border. The people in McBride had decided they'd had it with clear-cutting. They were tired of seeing the watershed destroyed and their pasture land ruined. They were largely a Mennonite community that staged one of the best conferences Merve had ever attended. Everyone got involved. The high-school students took part and one sixteen-year-old gave an excellent presentation on a community initiative to control the growth of underbrush in the forest. The community wanted to control the underbrush, not eradicate it. Their goal was to take all chemicals out of the forest. The boy's presentation told the story of how the community had cleared 3,000 acres the previous summer entirely by hand.

Normally the forestry service clears the brush by helicopter spraying. The community of McBride chose to do it with axes, scythes, and any other method that came to hand. The government offered no support for the town's initiative. They had a contract with Okanagan Helicopters and were determined to spray—or so they thought.

The mayor of McBride countered the government's spraying proposal with a simple rebuttal: "The helicopter won't fly," he said.

"How are you going to stop it?" they asked.

"We're not telling you now," the mayor replied. "That would be stupid. But we'll see that it does not fly. That's our watershed and we're not having it polluted with your chemicals when we have an alternative."

The government took the mayor seriously and backed down.

The people of McBride were bushmen, cattlemen, farmers, and youths who knew the woods well. They plotted their terrain onto graph paper and divided it up into one-acre lots. They labelled the plots difficult, intermediate, and easy. Then they went to the community and asked, "How many people want to take a hand in this project?"

Almost all the high-school kids signed on. Farmers, loggers, shopkeepers—everyone offered to lend a hand. When the organizers finished counting heads, they allotted the acres according to how difficult or easy the terrain was. This was paid labour, but organizers were determined to keep the cost of the project under the helicopter price. In the end, the project came in 10 percent under the cost of the helicopter, and everyone got a fair wage. One student estimated his average wage that summer was $12.50 per hour.

The government never chose to challenge the mayor of McBride. The mayor said he wouldn't have harmed anyone, but he was putting his foot down and he was going to sabotage the machine.

For Merve, the McBride initiative provided a real lesson in community effort.

At the conference, the town adopted several resolutions involving alternative methods of logging. As for the brushing-out of the land, the manager of the forest service in the area wrote a letter to Victoria saying he had inspected the operation and it had met every degree of his criteria and even exceeded it. He went on to write that he recommended this method as an economical way of doing brushing throughout British Columbia.

Merve's ideas were timely ones and well received in both Quesnel and McBride.

Of course I was well received. These individuals—who are only out for themselves—they don't attend these sorts of things. They sit on the outside. The public relations people never attend these things. They don't want to see it. If you don't see it, it doesn't exist. They have crazy ways of looking at it. You'll never get a forestry PR person to one of these meetings—certainly not here. It may happen in other countries but that I can't vouch for.

At the next conference he attended in Oregon in 1990, Merve received the Forester of the Year award, which he shared with a local forester, Orville Camp. He had been invited to the conference on reconstructive forestry to talk about what he was doing at Wildwood. On that occasion Merve was deeply impressed that nine top forestry people from the U.S. Forestry Service attended. It was the first time he had seen forestry people attend such a conference.

I was absolutely amazed at the frankness and the openness with which they discussed forest policy. They criticized their service like crazy, but it was constructive criticism. They weren't just knocking things down, they were calling for something that they thought was better. Then you had cross debate between the forest services from the different states ... And these fellows were excellent chairmen. They chaired a lot of our round table discussions and they didn't impose their ideas at all, but if there was something they felt would help, they would briefly outline it.

Also at this time schools started to come to Wildwood to learn about Merve's method of forestry. In particular, university classes were clamouring to visit his forest. The environmental class at the University of Victoria struck up an agreement with Merve to bring classes to Wildwood five or six times a year, for which Merve received

The horse loggers conference in Quesnel in 1986.

an honorarium and a payroll number on the university staff. The University of Oregon brought classes to Wildwood, as did the University of Washington and a number of colleges including Antioch College from New Hampshire. An enormous number of high schools brought classes. Even the Audubon Society made a field trip to Wildwood.

Europeans also started to arrive. The governments of Germany, France, Austria, Finland, Norway, Holland, Spain, and Switzerland sent foresters to Wildwood. Germany was particularly concerned with the failure of its monoculture system. In preparation for change, Germany sent scientists to Wildwood to study the soil and the entire biology of Merve's system.

These people are always looking for something that is different because they are trying to improve their forestry. And this is one thing that came out of that conference in Oregon: the willingness of their forestry people to listen to new ideas and experiment with them and try them out. That is not the attitude of forestry here. We don't want to hear. We don't want to know about it. They think you're attacking them when you're simply attacking their policy. It's not personal. You guys are great guys but for goodness sake—smarten up! You're going to waste our forests before you'll stop and listen.

At that Oregon conference, their attitude was that if you don't have the forest, you don't have anything. This I got from the Germans very clearly: If you don't have the forest, what good are your economics?

FROM ECO-FOREST TO CLASSROOM

In 1986, after Merve's appearance on Cam Cathcart's show, *Pacific Report*, Wildwood became a classroom. The transformation happened almost overnight. Thousands of groups have visited Wildwood since then.

Among the groups have been Girl Guides, Boy Scouts; elementary, high-school, and university classes; and a wide variety of environmental groups. Professional foresters from all over the world have come to study at Wildwood. Foresters have come from Germany, Holland, Finland, Norway, Sweden, Luxembourg, Switzerland, Spain, Jordan, France, Japan, China, Borneo, Java, Australia, Chile, Bolivia, Brazil, Costa Rica, Mexico, Cuba, Nigeria, and Libya. Foresters have also come to Wildwood from all parts of the United States.

Merve always greets them with unabashed joy. Whether it's a group of Grade 6 students or an official government delegation, he welcomes them with the same sincerity and the same eagerness to share his knowledge. He tells them that he has acquired some knowledge in his years of working in the forest, and he will answer their questions to the best of his ability, but if he does not know the answer he will tell them in plain English that he doesn't know. Merve won't invent fancy phrases to cover his ignorance. He is not ashamed to say he doesn't know, and if he knows where a person might get the answer to his question, he will refer them. "I don't know everything," he says. "But don't hesitate to ask the question and please keep it in plain language."

Plain language works. When he is working with people from another country, he has to work through a translator. Merve insists simple language works best even when English is your tongue. Phrases like "silvicultural prescription" mean nothing, he says. Only people who want to sound important make up such gobbledygook. And what about "site specific"? If site specific means that some trees will grow in one area and not in another, then say that: Don't say "site specific"! Pompous phrases accomplish only one thing: they shut out people who want to know.

Merve never talks down to anyone, not even the tiniest child. He never talks up to anyone either, no matter how impressive their name or position in society. Merve believes that children are smart and eager, and if they want to know about something he treats their questions with honesty and care.

The most important things Merve has learned about forestry are the following:

• The principle of sustainable forestry means keeping a tree of every age, size, and variety growing in the forest.

• When you choose the trees for a cut, you are selecting a volume that is less than the annual growth rate. You start by selecting trees that are windfalls—every forest produces the odd windfall. Then you select trees that may have died, weighing its value as a wildlife tree against its value as lumber. Keeping birds in the forest is a prime consideration. The third category includes trees that are beginning to fail; they are dying back and producing yellow needles.
These trees are producing wood slowly. They may take another 50 years to die and you are simply speeding up the process by taking them out. Always keep in mind that you want to leave enough dead trees for your wildlife habitat. After these

primary considerations, you should just take trees to thin the remaining forest, keeping in mind that you want to help the untouched trees grow tall and strong. Above all, you must not cut all one size of tree; it is imperative to keep diversity in the forest.

- Use the smallest equipment that will do the job. Large equipment damages the soil and the systems in the soil on which the tree depends. Merve recalls an experiment where he used a 30-horsepower cat one year and a 50-horsepower cat five years later. Using the larger cat was more expensive and gave a lower return.

- Be careful not to damage other trees when falling one. Learn to put your tree down where it will have minimum impact.

- Don't fall from early May until mid-June because that is when the birds are nesting. You can't see the nests from the ground but they are certainly there. Another factor at that time of year is bugs. In May and June the wood-boring beetles fly and lay their eggs. If you have timber on the ground you'll have pinworms in your logs.

- You'll do damage to the site if you take out long logs. Cut them down because the mill will anyway. Take out logs no longer than 16 to 26 feet.

- Be careful to maintain a network of seed trees spread over your property in such a way that the local winds will distribute the seeds. You will never have to plant trees. Seed trees should be clearly marked out. Merve has never planted a single tree at Wildwood other than those he has planted for experimental reasons.

- Minimize the size of your decks—a deck is a stack of timber. In other words, co-ordinate hauling the logs out with the transporting of them because big decks damage the land.

Chapter 20

A "Happening"

In October 1989, the Raging Grannies waltzed into Merve's life. The Raging Grannies are a group of women who got together in 1987 and quickly became as notorious a group of activists as were ever formed in British Columbia. Anne Pask was a Raging Granny pretty well from the start. Along with her friends, she popped up wherever the tone and spirit of the court jester would help the causes of peace and environmental responsibility.

Merve didn't know much about the Raging Grannies, but he liked what he'd seen on television and what he'd read about them in the news. He liked their flamboyant style and the clever songs they used to lampoon policies they deplored with. To Merve, the Raging Grannies represented a new trend: people who could laugh at themselves and use humour to get their point across.

Eco-forestry was one of the Raging Grannies' prime interests. When Merve hosted the State of the Islands Conference on sustainable forestry in October that year, the Raging Grannies asked to come. They termed their visit "research"; if they were going to protest something, they wanted to know what they were talking and singing about. But because they were engaged in another activist event on the day of the conference, they arranged to visit Wildwood the day before.

Nine Raging Grannies arrived on a typically wet, dreary October morning. Merve met the women at the gate at the top of his property. There wasn't a flower-bedecked hat to be seen, but Merve was taken with them anyway. This was one of the brightest and most upbeat bunch of women he'd seen. One in particular caught his eye: Anne Pask was bright and smart, smiling and laughing—the kind of person Merve gravitated to.

He toured the women around his forest and talked about his activities while the rain drizzled relentlessly down. At noon he invited them into his kitchen where they could enjoy their picnic lunch by the warmth of the woodstove. The conversation was lively, and when talk turned to some of Anne's exploits, Merve looked at her even more closely. He heard how Anne had joined a large party on a trip to the Carmanah Valley. She had walked across the clear-cut moonscape there and fallen in love with the old trees. The *Globe & Mail* newspaper had quoted her as saying, "They are our distant cousins in the ecological family and we ought to treat them as such."

For her part, Anne was intrigued with Merve. She liked his confident walk, his passion for the forest, his guileless eyes, and his easy courtesy. Something stirred in her. As the group left later that day, Merve and Anne's eyes met and held for just a moment. Back home, Anne volunteered to write a thank-you letter to Merve. Merve wrote back.

> *I said how much I'd enjoyed having them up and that I'd found them a very interesting group. I said I had a feeling I wanted to see more of her and as I was going to be in Victoria the next week, would she like to have lunch with me?*

Anne said yes, and Merve took her to the Princess Mary restaurant. They compared experiences and ideologies and found much in common. Anne had been raised on a prairie farm and had spent many years nursing in the communities of the far north. In her own way, she was as much a naturalist as Merve. Both were active for essentially the same causes.

By the end of the day, Merve was feeling the first beginnings of a romantic flutter. He knew he wanted to see more of Anne, but he was reluctant to jump in quickly. He had always been cautious in matters of the heart. Now, too, he tempered his emotions with hard-headed practicality. If anything was going to happen, he wanted to take it slowly. Anne liked Merve as much as he liked her and she was just as determined to be wary.

They began a courtship that lasted two years. They visited back and forth and wrote copious letters. During this time Merve succumbed to pressure from his many friends and acquaintances and co-wrote, with Ruth Loomis, *Wildwood*, the chronicle of his forest. It was an immensely popular book that found its way to Austria, China, Japan, India, and many parts of North America. The first edition sold out quickly and *Wildwood* went into a second printing.

In 1991 Anne travelled to Russia, and Merve made a canoe trip in the Yukon. When they returned they were reunited at the annual Peace Walk in Nanoose Bay, just north of Nanaimo, to protest the torpedo-testing range where the United States Navy in concert with the Canadian military had operated a submarine-testing base for years. A vocal group of environmentalists said the Navy had picked the Canadian location because no Americans would die in the event of a nuclear accident. It was a time of much rhetoric. Anne was there along with the other Raging Grannies. She had visited the Marshall Islands in the Pacific where the Americans had dropped their test bombs and had seen the human results of nuclear bombings. Merve was there because he hated the idea of nuclear submarines in his backyard. He also had reason to hate the test range because he believed that nuclear rain had killed Mary.

In December of that year, Anne invited Merve to be her guest at a reunion for people who had lived and worked in the Yukon. They danced the night away, towards a new beginning for both of them. Merve was 78 and Anne 73, and they might as well have been 50 years younger.

Maybe I wasn't as ardent as when I was twenty, and maybe it might take me a little longer to get excited. My emotions may have been a little more reserved, a little less exuberant, but they were more solid feelings. I wasn't as worried if I was doing the right thing. I had a sense of entry into the relationship with a more mature approach. I was not approaching the relationship with the idea we would be absolutely inseparable. I knew we would have differences of opinion, but I also knew we could handle them without antagonism.

Anne knew she was in love, but they had never talked about love. She'd heard Merve talk about his various female partners—paddling partners, dancing partners—and wondered how serious they were? She had never been married, although she had been engaged 35 years before. She'd had the wedding dress made and she was ready to walk down the aisle when she called it off. He was the wrong man, but it was the right dress, so she had it stored.

On December 28, Anne drove to Wildwood to have dinner with Merve and to meet Marquita. Merve had already made up his mind that the time was right to ask Anne to marry him, but before Marquita left that evening, she pulled Merve aside and said, "I really like her, Dad. She's very nice." His daughter's words confirmed his resolve.

Alone at last, Merve threw more logs on the roaring fire and sat down in his big old chair. Anne took a chair on the opposite side of the hearth. It wasn't a comfortable chair—not soft and padded like the one Merve was occupying—and that may have been cleverly designed. After watching Anne shift around, trying to get comfortable, Merve said, "How about coming over here? This chair is big enough for two."

Anne tucked herself in beside Merve, and he took her hand in his. "Would you consider getting married?" he asked.

"Yes," Anne said.

"Well how about next week?"

The wedding didn't take place until April 21. Events seemed to conspire to make the engagement a longer one than they wanted. First there was the court case Anne was involved in. The Vancouver Island Peace Council, of which Anne was a member, was suing the government for breaking its own environmental laws by allowing nuclear-powered ships to dock in Victoria's harbour. Anne had been selected as one of two members to represent the Peace Council's case in court. Then, a few days after announcing their engagement, Anne discovered a small bump in her breast. She knew Merve had lost his first wife to cancer and she didn't want him to feel that sort of pain again.

"You don't have to continue with this wedding," she told him.

Merve didn't give Anne's suggestion a single thought. "You go ahead with the surgery," he said.

She invited me to feel it and see for myself. And I thought, "My goodness, this is really, really fair. This is going far beyond what was necessary." I thought that was just wonderful of Anne.

Anne was fortunate. The bump was tiny and right near the surface. When the surgeon removed it in a lumpectomy at the end of January, he got it all.

With all that behind them, Merve and Anne began to prepare for the wedding in earnest. One thing Anne didn't have to worry about was her wedding dress—after 35 years it was still a perfect fit.

Two weeks before the wedding and two days before Chief Forester John Cuthbert was due to tour Wildwood, a pack of dogs got at Merve's sheep, killing all 21 of them. Merve was duly upset, but two things helped him pull it together and prepare for the visit of the government officials. First, he called upon his almost bottomless

Merve and Anne in a chair built for two—the perfect place to propose marriage!

reserves of inner strength and then he called on Anne. She dashed up to Wildwood to help out. Although Cuthbert was there under duress, his managers listened and seemed genuinely interested.

Immediately after the government visit, Merve went to Vancouver to make a presentation to Great Britain's Prince Philip, who was then the president of the World Wildlife Federation. MacMillan Bloedel had invited him to come to the West Coast to have a look at the good job they were doing of preserving the natural habitat while clear-cutting the forest. Prince Philip agreed to come but with the proviso that anyone could make a presentation to him.

So shortly before his wedding day, Merve travelled to Vancouver where he was one of 32 delegates to talk to Prince Philip about forest practices in B.C. Prince Philip heard one request over and over: Don't let yourself be given a snow job. When MacMillan Bloedel takes you up in the helicopter, don't let them fly too high or too low so that you won't be able to get a true picture of forestry in B.C.

Prince Philip addressed their concerns. "This is obviously something of much concern here in this meeting. May I assure you, I am not here to be given a snow job. I am here to look and see and think about what I have seen. If they fly me too high, I'll ask them to fly lower, please. If they fly me too low, I'll ask them to fly me higher, please. If they won't do either, I'll take the machine over and fly it myself."

His statement brought the house down and eased all fears and doubts about what he would and would not see. As it turned out, Prince Philip saw a great deal—a great deal that MacMillan Bloedel rather wished he had not. When he returned to England he made his report. At its kindest, his report called B.C.'s forestry practices disastrous and exceedingly destructive. Shortly after the report was published, Britain began to boycott British Columbian wood and wood products unless those products came from sustainable forests like Merve's.

Merve and Anne now barely had enough time to catch their breaths and dress for the wedding.

It was one of Victoria's social and media events of the year. Everyone who knew Merve and Anne was thrilled about the wedding. There were far too

Here comes the bride!

many people to invite formally, so drawing up a guest list proved a formidable task. They solved the problem by having a folk wedding and inviting everyone by simply asking them to come and then telling them to pass the news on to someone else. They requested no gifts— they had far too much of everything already—but said that a potluck dish would be very much appreciated.

When the numbers of people crowding into the First United Church in Victoria surpassed 300, they stopped counting. The minister observed more than once that it wasn't a ceremony but a happening.

Before the official kiss time, Anne got herself into a very tempting position, so I gave her a little peck, much to the amusement of the audience. "Oh that's not supposed to happen yet," the minister said … and then, "Oh well, this is a happening."

The Raging Grannies occupy the back rows
of the church while Merve and Anne exchange vows.

The happening kicked off with a choir procession to the front of the church. Merve and Anne followed behind them, walking down separate aisles to meet at the front of the church. It was arguable whether more eyes were on the bride or on the groom. Twenty-three Raging Grannies occupied the back pews. They were appropriately dressed in flowered hats and flowing shawls and carrying bumbershoots that later served as an honour guard on the church steps.

Earlier in the week, the Grannies had sent a press release to the media stating that the only unmarried Raging Granny was getting hitched, so reporters and news cameras added to the general melee.

Outside the church door at the end of the ceremony, the crowd spilled over the sidewalk and onto the street effectively shutting down rush-hour traffic. When a police cruiser was dispatched to move the crowd and saw what the holdup was, he quietly turned off his siren and lights and beetled down a side street to return on foot.

The reception in the church hall was pronounced by all to be the best wedding of the century. No icebreaker was needed to get the guests up on their feet and dancing to the music. There wasn't a wallflower in the place. The party ended with a sacred dance, the crowd forming a circle around two chairs set up for Merve and Anne. But before they could get started, one guest rushed in and took one of the chairs away.

"I heard you were short of furniture," the MC said in a toast to the bride. And Anne sat in Merve's lap as the laughing crowd danced around them.

The Raging Grannies form an honour guard for Merve and Anne.

| The happy couple at the reception. | Merve and Anne toast each other. |

For their honeymoon they took an idyllic trip down the coast of Washington State. Eight days later they sailed back to Victoria from Port Angeles, arriving at Wildwood two hours before Merve's first university class of the year and two days before a second wedding reception at their home for those who had not been able to make the trip to Victoria.

Chapter 21

Clayoquot Sound

The rumblings over Clayoquot Sound began in 1991, and by 1993 it was a full-blown crisis. Clayoquot Sound encompasses one of the largest tracts of temperate rain forest remaining in North America. It extends from Estevan Point on the west coast of Vancouver Island down to Pacific Rim National Park and encompasses nine major watersheds and several large islands. Its 2,440 square kilometres of lush rain forest are considered to be some of the most spectacular wilderness areas on the continent.

When Mike Harcourt's NDP government and MacMillan Bloedel announced they were going to clear-cut this precious jewel, it was no surprise to anyone that the environmentalists raised a clamour.

But the furor over Clayoquot Sound reached far deeper and wider than a handful of environmental protesters. The proposed rape of this pristine wilderness area raised the indignation of people on a nearly global level. Business people protested, people involved in tourism made their voices heard, and otherwise conservative people objected loudly to the proposal.

The traditional voices of protest were predictable in their anger, but at Clayoquot a new voice could be heard—the voice of people who wanted dialogue and a chance to reason with the government. "This plan is faulty," they said. "You're going to ruin a whole area that is priceless to the rest of the world. You can sell this area for tourism over and over again and you're going to ruin it for one cut of timber."

Merve's was one of the voices that pleaded for sanity. He invited the premier and his cabinet to come and look at his operation to show them that clear-cutting was unnecessary. The government refused to come. But then the NDP government had invested $90 million of pension money in MacMillan Bloedel stock. When queried by the media about the money, government officials said, "We don't tell the pension plan what to invest in."

My foot they don't tell them! They know what's going on. They can step in and say, "Hey, we don't think that's wise. You should look for something else." That was not done. They knew, and to say they didn't was a bit ridiculous.

The logging at Clayoquot Sound triggered the biggest incidence of civil disobedience Canada has ever known. People came from all over the country and all over the world to protest at Clayoquot Sound. An entire trainload of protesters arrived from the Maritimes. Some took time off work and some quit their jobs. They said that they came because the East Coast had been ruined. "For heaven's sake, please don't ruin the West."

Premier Harcourt refused to listen. From Merve's perspective that response could be traced directly to the human traits that he abhorred: stupidity, greed, selfishness, and plain bullheaded ignorance.

I was absolutely disgusted at a new government doing such an eminently stupid thing as one of the first things on its agenda. They had a chance to take a good look at it. They had recommendations in their hands because some of us made recommendations ahead of time that certainly should have justified a second look. But they insisted they weren't going to take a second look. That's what got people so steamed up. More than the plan was the absolute stonewalling by the government to any change whatsoever. I was really, really annoyed. I was disgusted at the shortsightedness of the government.

The protesters started their blockade of the logging road in June 1992. Thousands of people travelled to Tofino to take part. The people of Tofino were more than supportive because they depended on the tourist trade. They could expect upwards of 600,000 people a year to come to their town specifically to visit Clayoquot Sound. They rented canoes and kayaks and charter boats to the tourists. They fed them and they put them up in bed and breakfast establishments.

Visitors came for the incomparable scenery, the towering first-growth forests, and the abundant fishing. They came to photograph bears ambling along the beaches and to watch eagles soaring over the towering cliffs. The people who travelled to Clayoquot Sound believed it was an area of the world worth fighting for. By 1993, the backlash against clear-cutting had grown into a world movement. European countries were beginning to put an embargo on Canadian wood products in protest over clear-cutting.

People camped in the woods and on the beaches. They brought banners and placards. Each day they assembled on the Kennedy River bridge, which was the beginning of the logging road and the only access to Clayoquot Sound. Among the protesters were a group called The Friends of Clayoquot Sound and the Sierra Club. Even some NDP members of Parliament showed up to lend their support to the protesters.

Merve was as worked up as any of the protesters, but he took a different approach. He knew that "no logging" was a pipe dream, so he spearheaded a different movement. Instead of "no logging," he stressed "no clear-cutting" as an attainable goal. The first time he visited Clayoquot Sound was as a speaker invited by The Friends of Clayoquot Sound. Merve spoke eloquently and passionately but his passion was liberally laced with good common sense and an unstinting dedication to calling it like it is. He got his point across, and the battle cry of Clayoquot Sound became "No Clear-cutting!" instead of "No Logging!" and the placards were changed.

Meanwhile other activists educated the protesters about the essentials of non-violence and potential arrests. The protesters possessed the weapon of numbers. Each day as many as 1,200 protestors packed the bridge, and many were arrested. The reocrd was 308 arrests in one day, although those under the age of nineteen were allowed to go as soon as they had been removed from the site.

The media arrived and recorded it all. Everyone showed up: the European and South American press as well as the full gamut of North American press and TV reporters.

The government did its best to label the protesters a bunch of rabble-rousers. There were certainly a lot of young people, but also very prominent among the group were doctors, lawyers, school principals, teachers, professors, pastors, and middle-aged businessmen.

The chap who was standing beside me when we got arrested was one of the head English professors at UBC. The man was a perfect gentleman and exceedingly well educated. To call him a rabble-rouser was ridiculous.

The young people risked far more than the older folks. The RCMP took their pictures and later turned them over to MacMillan

Bloedel. They were literally putting their futures on the line. Blacklists were supposed to be illegal in Canada—the key phrase being "supposed to be."

On August 9, Merve and Anne took their turn on the bridge at five o'clock in the morning. They were near the back of the crowd that day—a crowd that numbered 680 strong. The police arrested the protesters front to back in rows. Those arrested were put on a bus and sent to the recreation hall in Ucluelet. The same bus shuttled back and forth, so it was a long, painful process—especially since most of the protesters refused to walk on to the bus and had to be carried and there were only eight RCMP officers to handle the entire operation.

The arresting officers had a large audience of about a thousand people who had gathered around to watch. By the time the bus was due to come back for its last load of prisoners, only four officers were left on the bridge—four against a thousand.

Merve noticed that one of the young officers seemed to have assessed the odds. He didn't look particularly nervous, but he had begun pacing restlessly back and forth on the bridge, stopping every now and then to cast a baleful eye down at the running water below. Almost at a signal, a large group of spectators moved closer to the young policeman until they had him enclosed in a circle. When the circle was complete, they raised their voices in the Gilbert and Sullivan ditty "A Policeman's Lot is not a Happy One." The young officer broke up in helpless laughter.

Merve's arrest was as pleasant as an arrest can possibly be.

The officer walked up to him. "Are you prepared to step aside?" he asked.

"No," Merve replied. "I've been here the better part of the day now and I'll stay here until midnight if necessary."

"I'll have to arrest you then," the officer said.

"Well and rightly so," Merve said.

"Do I have to carry you?" he asked.

"No, you've already carried enough people today," Merve said. "I'll walk."

"Thank you," the officer said. "I appreciate that."

Merve and Anne got on the bus without assistance.

The recreation hall in Ucluelet was packed with protesters. The 300 minors were told to go as soon as the last busload arrived, but it was still a tight squeeze with over 300 people in the room. The crowd was in a festive mood. They'd gotten themselves arrested voluntarily and they were definitely pleased about it.

When the senior officer tried to make an announcement, the roar of happy chatter drowned him out. One of the detainees, noticing the man's dilemma, suggested, "Just put your hand up."

The officer looked skeptical but tried it. He raised his hand in the air and had their attention instantly. He was surprised, but not too surprised. He'd made enough arrests by now to know these weren't the rabble-rousers of the government's myth.

It took hours to process those in the gym. Thanks to a young couple who gave up their place in line, Merve and Anne were through the procedure by 6:30 that evening, but instead of heading straight home, they drove back to Tofino for a bite of supper and to fill the tank with gas. The proprietor of the café recognized them and took 50 percent off their bill. The gas station manager gave them the same discount. His reason was simple. "You're defending my business," he said.

Two months later, Merve was still waiting to hear about a trial date when he had to take a trip to Portland, Oregon, where he had accepted a two-week teaching position at the school of eco-forestry.

The protesters had been arrested on civil charges, but a few days later the government had converted them to criminal charges. Merve was quite clear in his mind that there would be problems at the border crossing. When a Canadian citizen enters the United States to work, he must answer a list of 50 questions. One of those questions is, "Have you ever been arrested on a criminal charge?"

Merve could easily have floated through customs, but that was not his way. He arrived at the Vancouver Airport well ahead of time. He hung back at the customs gate until he found an officer free and had no one waiting in line behind him. He was being considerate but he was also relishing the moment. Merve was going to have some fun.

The immigration officer ran through the usual questions: Citizenship? Purpose of visit?

"I'm not a tourist," Merve said clearly. "I'm going down to teach at the eco-forestry school in Oregon for two weeks. It is a paying job—an honorarium."

"That's very decent of you to mention it," the officer said and pulled out the long list of questions, apologizing that he had to go to the trouble.

"No trouble," Merve said. "I understand."

The questions ran down smoothly and finally he came to the one. "Have you ever been arrested on a criminal charge?"

"Yes, I have," Merve replied. "Very recently I was arrested for standing on the bridge and blockading Clayoquot Sound."

The customs man didn't miss a beat. "Good for you. We won't say anything about that." He stamped the papers and moved Merve on.

The Clayoquot Sound cases went to court late that year. Merve took a keen interest in the proceedings. He had been a technical witness in several lower court cases in the past and had developed a real respect for the judges. He had seen them do a conscientious job in trying to arrive at the truth and hand down a fair decision. The Supreme Court was another matter altogether.

It put me in touch with what happens in our Supreme Court. When I saw what the group of people was doing, it made me feel awfully good about being on the wrong side of the fence. It made me feel good about tackling something that was corrupt. The way the court system worked in regards to the protesters was a blot in the eye of justice. It proved that the removal of any suggestion of the word "justice" some 40 years ago from our law system was an indication of things to come.

Stink bombs used to be banned at one time. A truckload would have been in order in this case—delivered to the Legislature and split with the Supreme Court. All of it smelled and smelled badly.

During the trial it gradually became apparent that irregularities had occurred in the proceedings until then. The protesters had staged a civil disobedience on land open to the public and on a road paid for by the taxpayers either by direct grant or by reduced stumpage. There was no violence nor had there been any threat of violence. The only people who were injured were two female protesters hit by a drunken logger who drove his truck into the peace camp. No charges were ever laid in that case.

Merve and Anne were arrested August 9 with a group that included a university professor, a doctor, a bank manager, and a minister. Eight days after the arrest, the charges were changed to criminal charges by the Attorney General's office. If the charges had remained civil, the province could have avoided a large legal bill and MacMillan Bloedel would have had to process each and every case of breaking an injunction. The government neatly took the onus off the giant forest company, paid all the legal bills out of the public coffer, then quietly reversed the entire thing back to a civil action at the end of the trials.

Can you see MacMillan Bloedel processing a thousand civil suits? The whole thing would have blown up in their face. And then we might have gotten some better forestry as a bonus.

As soon as the processing had started at the school gym in Ucluelet the irregularities began. The group was told that the phone was out of service; no one could phone a lawyer. Later in the day, someone managed to slip by the police to the telephone. When he picked it up, he heard a normal dial tone.

Everyone had expected a mug shot to be taken, but in this case a second set of pictures was taken with a Polaroid camera. These were then given to MacMillan Bloedel so they could identify the protesters. The company had not made provisions for its own observers.

Under questioning in court, one of the staff sergeants admitted that in 32 years of service he had never seen this done. As far as he was concerned it was completely irregular. His testimony suggested that a second staff sergeant in Ucluelet started the process. He had just followed along. At the same time in the upstairs courtroom, the second staff sergeant offered similar comment but attributed the strategy to the officer in the courtroom down below.

Under questioning, the personnel manager at the Clayoquot MacMillan Bloedel operation admitted he received a case of Polaroid photos from the police.

"And what did you do with these pictures?"

"I went straight to the office with them."

"Did you go straight to the office? Did you stop anywhere between the police station and the office?"

The manager admitted he had stopped at the Potbelly Café, the headquarters for the loggers in the area.

"Were there other people in the café?"

"Oh yes."

"What did you do with the photographs?"

"I kept them on my person even when I went to the bathroom."

"Are you absolutely sure that those pictures remained inside the container?"

The man didn't want to lie. "Well. Some of them did get out on the table."

Under closer questioning, it turned out that many of the photos managed to get out on the table where all who were present and curious got a good look at them. So much for the B.C. Privacy Act.

With hundreds arrested, mass trials were decided upon—a real black eye for justice. Groups of up to 40-odd. The rights under Canada's laws were allowed to be discarded. We had no rights under Canada's Charter of Rights. When you are charged with a criminal act, you have the right to a jury. That was denied immediately. Freedom of assembly was pretty well scrapped in this case, and the Privacy Act was cancelled by the photo exchange.

The judges ranged from very decent fellows like Judge Skipp, who allowed witnesses, to the exact opposite. The court order that allowed the whole thing to happen wouldn't exist in other countries.

The protesters were there to protest an injunction that was so sweeping it could criminalize the public for simply having knowledge of it. The final phrase of the injunction read: "... and all others having knowledge of the injunction."

Judge J. Bouck, the man who had originally issued the injunction, had been on the legal staff of MacMillan Bloedel just before he was appointed to the Supreme Court. Prior to the blockade, he took the original injunction and reworded it to include the infamous closing phrase, making anyone guilty who had knowledge of the injunction.

Did the knowledge make them guilty? If so, of what? Guilty of the injunction? Guilty of the knowledge of B.C.'s lousy logging? Guilty of knowledge of our justice system? What would you be guilty of in this particular case?

On the heels of the incredible followed the unthinkable. Justice Bouck was given the largest group in the first mass trial. It fell to Bouck to set precedents. Most of the accused could not afford a lawyer, so they defended themselves. But various defendants hired some dozen lawyers who were only too pleased to give unlimited free advice.

If not for the presence of the lawyers, a lot of the skullduggery in the case may well have remained hidden. Most of the judges disallowed witnesses. One judge ruled that each defendant had only three minutes to make a statement and another allowed all of five minutes.

Merve was on hand for the opening day in court because he had been called as a technical witness. His own trial was set for a later date. The lawyers had managed to get a few technical witnesses on the agenda with the premise that the defendants had a right to cross-examine a witness.

Bouck entered a packed courtroom. There were 43 defendants, the Crown prosecutor, half a dozen lawyers, a mass of spectators, and a full press gallery. The judge, fully aware that the recording of proceedings would not start until he said the words, "I declare this court in session," came in, stood, looked down at the crowd, and said, "I don't care what any of you say, you're all guilty." He then sat down, declared the court open, and stated that the group could not call any witnesses.

One lawyer stood up and said, "This is completely unconstitutional, Justice Bouck. I don't think you can get away with it."

"This is a mass trial," Bouck countered. "This procedure hasn't been used in Canada."

"Yes it has been used in Canada before, Justice Bouck, in the Winnipeg riot of 1912."

Bouck had a bit of backtracking to do. He ended up ruling that the group could still not call a witness, but an individual could. The argument took up the entire morning. As soon as Bouck ruled on the individual witnesses, the same lawyer moved for a lunch break. Bouck was only too glad to agree.

The lawyers and defendants adjourned to the restaurant across the street for a war conference. The lawyers briefed the men and women as to who and what they were up against. They also concocted a scheme they felt might work. One of the men in the group, George Harris, suggested that he call his witness, who was Merve. Then, once that witness was on the stand, couldn't he be a witness for the whole group and be questioned by the group?

"Technically you're right," the lawyer said. "He may try to override that, but give it a try."

When court was called to order after lunch, the first defendant called his first witness. Merve took the stand and happily answered the leading questions.

"Do you consider blockades should be necessary rather than the establishment of a good forestry policy?"

"The establishment of a good forestry policy would have such tremendous benefits it would prevent the very thing we're involved in today. Blockades just wouldn't be necessary."

Sixteen questions later, the defendant thanked Merve, turned to the court, and said, "As Justice Bouck will admit, you are all now open to use my witness."

Bouck let it go but he got his revenge. He let Merve talk for the rest of the afternoon, but while Merve talked, Bouck pulled out a magazine—some said it was *Playboy*—and read it with great interest.

He paid no attention whatsoever. That was his way of going on strike. I don't know if I made a remark at the end of the day about a legal blockade ... I very well could have. I had good questions coming at me all day. I was having a wonderful time, but I was fighting mad too, and absolutely disgusted. My disgust at the end of that afternoon for the justice system was as high as Mount Everest. If I could have dumped the mountain on Bouck, I would have done so. And there were others like him. He was not the only one.

By the second day of the trial, Bouck had blocked all witnesses.

✳ ✳ ✳

Merve and Anne's day in court came on January 9, 1994. Judge Skipp opened proceedings by looking down on his group of 28 defendants and telling them he had no choice but to find them guilty.

But Skipp's kindly face and open demeanour endeared him to Merve instantly. Here was a man he could like—a man who seemed to be the polar opposite of Judge Bouck.

Merve and Anne were among twelve people in the group who had elected to defend themselves. The first thing Merve did was ask for a trial by jury. Skipp explained that that section of the Charter of Rights had been abrogated, so there would be no trial by jury.

Then Anne made a request. Because of sheer numbers the defendants were seated in the spectators' section. That was fine for most, but Anne couldn't hear, so she asked the judge if she could sit in an empty chair beside the row of lawyers.

Skipp suggested that Anne and anyone else having trouble hearing should come up and sit in the jury box. Ten defendants took Skipp up on his offer. From there, they had a perfect vantage point. Not only could they hear well, but they could see every nuance of expression in the lawyers' and witnesses' faces.

Skipp had given the defendants the right to cross-examine witnesses. If they weren't sure of how to go about that, the judge coached them. He also allowed the defendants to take full advantage of one item in the Charter of Rights that had not been shut off—*mens rhea*—meaning "frame of mind." In other words, Skipp allowed the defendants to explain their frame of mind in detail: why they were at the scene, what their intent was, and all the reasons and thinking behind their actions. He gave the 28 people in his courtroom carte blanche to state their case and he gave each defendant his undivided attention.

When his turn came up, Merve told the judge why he had gone to Clayoquot Sound—not just to take part in the blockade and to be arrested, but also to speak to the group about proper methods of forestry. He told the judge that one of his aims had been to swing the group away from a "no logging" mindset to a "no clear-cutting" paradigm.

> *I made my case for having been arrested. I told the judge why I considered that important. It was necessary in the overall picture of trying to make progress in forestry. I stated my case quite clearly and told him that I had no regrets whatsoever. I told him that I went up there to attract more attention to the fact. I knew people were watching to see what I was going to do. I wanted to let people see in no uncertain terms that I was quite willing to put my feet where my mouth is. I was willing to get out there and do something about it—not just talk about it.*

Of course the entire group was found guilty. When Merve got his last chance to speak before sentencing was handed down, he quoted his grandfather. "If you meet a problem, face it. If you get knocked down in the process, stand up for what you believe, and face it again." And then he ended by saying he had no regrets and was quite ready to do the same thing again. The judge said very little in reply, but in his written judgment that was entered into the court records, Skipp ended his assessment of Merve Wilkinson by calling him "magnificently unrepentant."

Merve and Anne were handed the two stiffest sentences in their group: 100 hours of community service each. But Skipp was so clearly and obviously fair and helpful that when he had finished and rose from his bench for the last time to leave his courtroom, the defendants spontaneously stood and gave him a resounding ovation.

Skipp had shown his humanity every day. When Merve had to absent himself for a day early on in the proceedings because he had to attend a sick sheep, Skipp very kindly asked after the sheep the next morning. At the same time as the court case was going on, vandals were targeting Merve: his gate was damaged, his fence broken, and four of his lambs brutally mutilated. When the Victoria newspaper carried the story of the damage and included the fact that Merve had taken to carrying a shotgun and was not afraid to use it, the vandalism stopped as quickly as it had begun. At exactly the same time, the IWA issued a press release saying that tempers were running rather high and it was time for things to cool down.

With the trial over, Merve reported to the Nanaimo probation office to begin his 100 hours of community service. The man in the office was one of the stuffy, brassy types that could so easily aggravate Merve.

"How are you going to work off the hours?" the man asked.

Merve said. "I'm teaching alternative forestry on a voluntary basis to the schools in Nanaimo. I can double up on that and also take classes to the schools where I know they don't have time to come to me."

"We can't have you doing that," the man said.

"Who are 'we'?" Merve asked.

The man gave Merve a baleful stare and asked, "You're in forestry?"

"Yes."

"Do you know how to operate a power saw?"

"Yes."

"Would you cut wood for the needy?"

"Gladly. M&B has a huge slash pile of debris out on the Nanaimo Lakes Road. If they'll give me access to that pile, I'll gladly cut the wood. I'll even pay for the gas."

"They wouldn't like that," the man said.

"Well, they're only going to burn it."

"Any other suggestions?"

"Well, one place that always needs volunteers is the Morrell Sanctuary. There are things I can do to help them."

"That would be excellent," the man said. "That's apolitical."

Merve put in his 100 hours helping to set up a woods interpretive centre at the sanctuary. In fact, it added up to 101 hours. They were one hour short of finishing when Merve's time was up. But as he said to the rest of the crew, he wasn't the sort of man to drop a case of dynamite in the munitions factory just because the whistle blew for five o'clock.

By now he had become friendly with Heather, the supervisor at the probation office. When he arrived for the last time, old fish-eye—as Merve had come to think of him—was there as well.

"Merve, have you got your hours all filled in?" Heather asked.

"Yes, I do," he said. "And I've even got an extra hour banked against the next blockade."

Fish-eye left, slamming the door behind him.

Anne had a more difficult time doing her hours. By this time film crews were swarming around the place and she barely managed to get in two hours at a time in the local intermediate care facility. Every day for weeks some member of the media was knocking at their door. They had learned about Merve and his "unrepentant" stance through the court case. He had become one of the "stars" of the blockade. He was not only the man who stood up for his beliefs; he was also the forester who knew a better way to do it.

The public service television networks from the United States and from South America filmed at Wildwood. The BBC from Britain and film crews from Germany also arrived. Because he'd got himself arrested at Clayoquot Sound, Merve's stature had grown to international levels.

Merve and Anne host the International Conference of Eco-Forestry, September 1999.

Merve with Gareth Davies, a forestry student from Eastern Canada. Davies is one of countless young people who have come to Wildwood to study sustainable forestry.

Chapter 22

The Work Continues

Marriage came easy for Anne and Merve. They fit together. They shared values and viewpoints, a love of life, and a respect for the environment. As with all marriages, there was a small period of adjustment, but in their case, Anne did most of the adjusting.

Merve was used to the endless stream of visitors that came to Wildwood from all over the world. For Anne it meant hard work. Every week brought either a film crew, a foreign delegation, a group of students, a gang of would-be eco-foresters, or any number of their large collection of friends and relatives. Many of them didn't just come for the day; they stayed for a weekend or longer.

What brought them all to Wildwood? One day Merve posed the question to a German forester, who explained it this way: "We know what happens with this kind of management in 10 years and 20 years, but you have been managing the land for 50 years. We want to see what it's like in the long term where one man—not a government, not a corporation, not a society, not even a family— carries through this operational plan."

"How do you like what you see?" Merve asked him.

"I love it," he replied.

Robert Bateman, the acclaimed wildlife artist, became a frequent visitor. In fact, Bateman came with one of the first environmental groups from Saltspring Island.

The meeting between Bateman and Merve was one that Merve remembers well.

He's one of these people—like Jane Goodall and many many others— where right away there's something electric that takes place between you. You say, "Hey, I like you" inside yourself because of the way you speak to each other, by the interests you share, and by the values you share.

Merve with his friend Robert Bateman. Both men were honoured with the Order of British Columbia at Government House in Victoria, June 20, 2001.

Bob Bateman paints magnificent pictures of wild creatures as if you were right there next to the animal. He has done well with his art— it's alive! But far more important to him is his effort to save the habitat of the creatures he has come to love.

Bateman and Merve met when they found themselves speaking at the same conference. After that they met socially through friends they had in common. It was both fitting and widely applauded when both men were announced as 2001 recipients of the Order of British Columbia.

Wilkinson brought down the house during his investiture when he stood on the stage and stuck his thumb victoriously in the air as the master of ceremonies read, "Merve Wilkinson began harvesting trees at Wildwood, his 138-acre property, in 1945. Now, over 50 years later, he still has the same amount of timber he started with."

Even Premier Gordon Campbell and Lieutenant-Governor Garde B. Gardom applauded the gesture and joined in the laughter.

For Wilkinson's friends who attended the ceremony the "thumbs-up" gesture was particularly significant because Wilkinson has been thumbing his nose at the established forestry industry for almost 60 years.

Wilkinson later confessed that as he shook hands with the new premier he told him, "You know, you boys ought to give this sustainable forestry a try."

It was natural for a mutual respect and friendship to develop between the artist and the eco-forester. It was just as natural for a friendship to develop between Merve and Jane Goodall. Goodall arrived at Wildwood in 1997 as a member of the LIFE flotilla. LIFE (Leadership Initiative For Earth) is an organization that puts young people on tall ships along with elders as part of an environmental learning experience for the young people. Wildwood is one of the flotilla's regular ports of call.

Merve also experienced that meeting of kindred souls with Jane Goodall, but it wasn't until she had been at Wildwood for two hours that he made a mental connection and realized, "Oh, this is *that* Jane Goodall."

Jane Goodall stands as one of the great scientists of our time. Her hard work with the chimpanzees has forced human beings to recognize they are not the only ones who feel pain and real emotions. Jane has also found it necessary to spend much of her time and efforts fighting against habitat destruction and animal abuse.

Jane Goodall was so taken with Wildwood she came back a few months later to spend a weekend and really explore the forest.

Merve and Anne's involvement with David Suzuki began when the David Suzuki Foundation was just getting started. Merve sent a donation and a letter, offering to help out with Wildwood as an educational forum. David Suzuki took Merve up on his offer. He went to Wildwood, first to film a two-hour TV special, "Spirit of the Forest," then to film two more shows, "Battle of the Trees" and "Merve's Forest." The latter was a film for and by children. It was during the filming of the children's special that Merve came to appreciate Suzuki, the man.

It is so easy for people who are important and who have a lot of knowledge to take over. Other than suggesting a question, he never once tried to take over from the kids. He was in the background to give advice and to direct the camera, but it was the kids' show. And I thought, by Jove, this marks out a big man. Because it's so easy for all of us to take over, particularly when there are gaps. And there were gaps; they were just youngsters of twelve and thirteen.

Jane Goodall talks with Merve on a visit to Wildwood in April 2001.

In 1996, David Suzuki founded the Council of Elders. Merve and Anne were the only founding members living outside Vancouver. Suzuki had had the idea for the Council of Elders for some time. Having looked at Aboriginal cultures and cultures of peoples all over the world, Suzuki had come to the conclusion that the white culture was the only one that did not revere and respect its elders. Instead of learning from the elders, the white culture tended to shunt them aside, and each generation had to learn the same things for themselves over and over again. It seemed to Suzuki that the wisdom of the elders was more necessary than ever. Since the Second World War, technology had changed so rapidly that the younger generation had no first-hand experience of what the world was like a mere twenty years before; that experience was known only to the elders. Suzuki's Council of Elders was intended to be one step toward changing how North American culture views its seniors.

Giving seminars at Wildwood became routine for Merve, but every now and then there was a standout. One day Merve hosted a conference for 92 students and professional foresters from 23 countries.

They had very intricate questions and very deep questions. They wanted to know how to go about fitting this system to their country and so on. They all were very appreciative. They took notes, and unlike our forestry people, they listened. They didn't shut their minds down so they couldn't hear what was being said.

These were people who were in the finishing and trading business, but they all had forestry degrees. They were here to buy goods if they were properly produced. They were here in order to encourage an interest in their secondary wood products that they wanted to export. There are people out there willing and ready to trade, but they will do it on their terms—one of their terms being absolutely no clear-cutting!

I turned down an order worth $5 million because I didn't have the material. But I knew about and told them about a side hill in Jervis Inlet where there was enough of that quality of wood rotting because the loggers had clear-cut. They didn't want the hemlock so they left it; they only took the cedar and the fir. There was enough timber on that hillside to satisfy that order and two or three more like it. This shows the stupidity of our forestry people here.

I can't take credit for having said this, but I'd like to: "They're so dumb that they don't know they're dumb."

Over the years, Merve developed a keen eye for what he called "corporate propaganda." One of the worst pieces he came across was MacMillan Bloedel's "Forests Forever" advertising campaign. The company spent $1.5 million on three television commercials. More were planned, but the public outcry cut the campaign off at the knees.

The first commercial was filmed on central Vancouver Island at Cathedral Grove, a small section of forest on MacMillan Bloedel lands where the old giants had been allowed to remain standing. To lend the scene just the right mood, the producers used a stuffed deer with glass eyes.

It was standing in a pose that no intelligent deer would ever stand in. I've seen hundreds of deer in my lifetime in the woods and you would just never catch a buck standing in that position.

The crew continued on to Port Alberni and filmed a young forest near Sproat Lake. The area had been razed by fire 90 years earlier and had grown up again through natural regeneration. The commercial presented the planting as the kind resulting from current forestry practices.

Their next stop was Dickson Lake, a lake whose natural beauty still managed to glow through the devastating clear-cut all around. A professional actor was posed in front of the only small grove of

Wildwood is a forum for Merve's philosophy, and no group comes to Wildwood without hearing it. It's a simple philosophy. Merve points out that it feels good to work with nature, to earn a living from the forest, and to not destroy the forest in the process. When you can live that way, you go home at night happy with what you have accomplished. You may be tired but you are not tense. You don't need a stiff drink and some quiet time. You don't feel like yelling at your spouse and children. When the children run to meet you, you're ready to hug them and play with them.

That's the small philosophical picture.

The big picture Merve talks about is the world. When you take trees out of the forest selectively, you leave a forest behind you, not a naked hillside. You leave a forest where the birds are still singing all around you. Merve likes to tell of the year when the grouse were nesting late. He felled a tree within six feet of a grouse's nest, but she never left her eggs. Merve suspended falling until the grouse had hatched her eggs and left the nest two weeks later. He knew that if one grouse was still nesting, there were countless others.

By practising selective logging he is saving the climate, wind patterns, wildlife, and the whole complicated chain of the natural environment. And by keeping the balance of the ecology in one small part of the world, Merve believes he is leading a fight to save the whole world.

Some people think only in terms of economics. To them, Merve says selective logging provides a constant supply of raw material tailored to suit what the earth can produce. What is needed may have to be tailored to fit what can be produced. It makes more sense than running out of raw materials. Selective logging produces a steady economy and a stable population that doesn't have to move because the jobs have disappeared. This, says Merve, is stability in economics, and "If you have fault to find with that, I have fault to find with you."

second-growth trees left standing and told the camera how pleased he was that he'd been a part of planting those trees.

One of the commercials showed an eagle flying in an arc. "Eagles don't fly in arcs," Merve thought as he watched the ad. "They don't fly at that speed and they certainly don't fly without moving their wings or feathers."

To Merve's immense joy, he wasn't the only person watching those ads who cried out against them. Most importantly, it was the younger generation that the forest companies couldn't fool. As more and more classes of elementary and high-school students came to Wildwood, Merve's faith in the younger generation grew.

Shortly after the Forests Forever campaign began to air, a high-school student from Parksville on a tour of Wildwood commented on the phony deer. Another from Ladysmith commented on the fake eagle.

A month later, Merve sat on a panel at a forum debating MacMillan Bloedel's second plan to log the Carmanah Valley. The second plan was better, but still not acceptable, and he told them so. "I'll grant you this, your second plan safeguards more of the valley, but you still propose to clear-cut and any clear-cutting in that valley is disastrous. And … to be really nitty-gritty about this: If we can't trust your advertising, can we trust your plans? If you are trying to dupe us as you tried to do with 'Forests Forever'—where you used a stuffed deer, second-growth that was planted by nature and not by you, and Mr. Dawson standing at Dickson Lake telling us what a wonderful job he did, what can we believe? Tell Mr. Dawson to go back and finish your job. He made one helluva mess."

Merve had no sooner finished his speech than a man in the audience of the packed hall jumped to his feet and began shouting, "He's right! I've been there! It's a helluva mess!" The man must have had his opinions bottled up for weeks. Once he got started he didn't stop. "Those trees are only 30 years old and he's talking about 50…." No one tried to stop him. The audience just clapped and laughed and nodded approval.

In 1995, *Wildwood*, the book, went into its second printing. The book's validity and reason for being had grown immensely in the five years since it was first published.

By the time 1990 hit it became obvious that there was so much interest for so many people in so many places. There was tons of mail coming in—people wanting more details: How did I start? Where did I start? What was it like to step out of the regular channels and do something different? Did it pay? There were literally hundreds of good, valid questions. Was it possible in all terrains? Was it possible in hardwood? These questions were coming in from the United States, from Japan, from South America, and from Mexico. Several people were saying, 'For goodness sake, Merve, get this down. Get this written.'

There was a tremendous amount of pressure to do the book, and after the book, there was a tremendous amount of pressure to do a video, and then a second video.

What I wanted to do was get out of forestry dogma and forestry jargon so that people could read it. From my own experience, I have found that the professional forestry people were creating meaningless jargon so that people didn't know how to go about questioning them. I have always welcomed questions and I think that anybody that's trying to accomplish something likes questions. Out of questions come ideas and sometimes those ideas are worth taking note of and even doing something about. You're a fool if you don't like questions. You're dishonest if you don't try to answer them. I don't have the answer to everything and I tell people that. If I don't have the answer I'll tell people I don't know.

When Anne came to Wildwood, she became an integral part of the operation. Merve had been giving workshops for years. One day, the organizers of a workshop on Pender Island asked Anne if she would speak. Anne talked about the spiritual values of the forest and the trees. Her speech touched the sentiments of many people there. It became part of the workshops and even influenced the way Merve looked after his trees.

Merve had always been thoughtful and conscious about choosing the trees he was going to fell. He never felled a tree without first asking himself why. Why this particular tree? Is this the right tree to fell? In later years, in the same way the Aboriginal elders spoke to the trees and asked their permission before felling, he got in touch with his own deep feelings toward the trees.

You're respecting the tree. It's a living thing. You're addressing it; they understand and know you're thinking about what you're doing.

Wildwood is a success story, not only in forestry, but as a
testament to humans living with nature and not upsetting the
balance. Today Wildwood is guaranteed its future as a classroom
for generations to come. The British Columbia Land Conservancy
purchased the property in early 2001 from Merve and Grace with
the proviso that Merve and Anne will live out their days in their
forest. Wildwood will remain as natural as possible, but will be used
as an educational and experimental facility as well.

Merve will receive 25 percent of the purchase price of
$1,010,000. Merve's first action after the sale was to announce
that he would donate $150,000 back to the Land Conservancy.

Death holds no fear for Merve. Although he has lived with his
ideals, he is the consummate realist.

*Nothing goes on forever, but you make the most of every hour that
you have. Make the most of every hour, do the things that you like to
do, but primarily—for goodness sake—think of other people and
how your actions affect them, and how you can help them to be
better people.*

Merve relishes his role as an elder. Young people come to him
for advice. The questions vary but the answer is often the same: No
matter what your parents want for you or what other people want
for you, if you don't do what makes you happy, you will lead a very
unhappy life.

In this last phase of his life, Merve believes it is his duty to pass
on his knowledge in order to preserve it for generations to come.

*And you have to encourage your students to go further, not to stop.
There's an old saying that's been around for some time but it's one
of the most valid ones that I've ever come across: "You can't help
your neighbour to the top of the hill without getting there yourself."
And that is something I really believe in.*

*This kind of forestry has been very rewarding in that I know in
myself that I'm not destroying anything. I'm destroying one individual
tree, but I've thought about it and the tree is aware of it.*

*I've had the satisfaction of having done a job as I saw it and
enjoyed it without destroying the environment in which I did it.*

Epilogue

Now in his late 80s, Merve Wilkinson has barely slowed down his pace. His back stoops a little, and his hands are gnarled from years of curling them around a chainsaw and fighting against its vibrations. In July 1998 he fractured his right hip, and the replacement was not an immediate success. Despite two painful repairs to the hip replacement, Merve is still astoundingly active around his property.

His greatest work is teaching. Thousands of young people make the pilgrimage to Wildwood each year. Merve speaks with a passion about the need to preserve the earth.

On March 27, 1999, a tree fell in Merve's forest. Almost 300 people heard the sound and the words of blessing that accompanied it:

I have listened to the voice of time and have heard the elements sing—and now I know that my spirit will pass on. It will glide through the waters and fly with the wind—and follow the path of the stars. The end of my life will lead to the beginnings of others. My spirit will travel on: the cycle complete and within the future again, we all will meet.

The falling marked the beginning of the construction of Lifeship 2000, an ecologically built tall ship that will serve as the expedition vessel for LIFE (Leadership Initiative For Earth). The ship will travel the world, spreading its message of peace and sustainable living on the planet.

At the ceremony, Merve said, "The ship is to be built as near as humanly possibly with the minimum amount of damage to the environment. We live on an expendable planet and we've been expending it at an alarming rate. Today, young people by the hundreds and thousands are saying 'No, we've had enough of this. We want to live on an earth that's beautiful and where we can make a living without destroying it.'"

A deck of logs waiting to be milled at the mill site on Merve's property.

In 1999, Merve received a standing ovation in the ballroom of the Hotel Vancouver at the Ethics in Action Awards dinner where he was given a special achievement award.

And he just keeps on going. His focus is on the present rather than on the future. And much of that present focus bemoans the state of the earth and mankind.

You have this progress going on and constant change. Evolutionary changes come so slowly that they don't disrupt. But the changes that we as so-called civilized people cause ... we are anything but civilized in the way we behave towards other nations, other races, other cultures, other religions, and sometimes even our next-door neighbours. We are far from civilized. It's time we learned to be civilized and time our business leaders learned to be civilized—and also honest for a change. Honesty was a large part of our growing-up process. We seem to have discarded it for the dollar.

Anne and I can see a lot of our own past in the present: how we grew up and the things that shaped our lives. The values are still there but in a lot of cases they are watered down. Our younger people now— and I can say this without the least hesitation—are wanting to get back to those standards. They don't necessarily want to turn back the hands of time, but to be able to apply the standards under which we grew up to the present-day world. There is a tremendous need and I see it more and more daily. They are wonderful young people but they are lost because society gives them no values and the government gives them nothing in the way of objectives to go for. And so many of our philosophical organizations have broken down, too, and are not staying with basic truths. There's a real need to bring back the ethics, the standards, and the degrees of honesty that were present in the past.

I had mentors. In my age group I think we had the benefit of more good mentors than people have today. They had standards: honesty meant honest, truth meant truth. Your responsibility to your fellow man was recognized. In my life I have had the privilege of knowing a number of magnificent people. My grandfather and my parents were the best of mentors. They pointed out in kindly, firm and convincing ways what was good and what was not good—how one should relate to their fellow man, and how one should not relate to their fellow man. I give credit to them for the basics in my makeup and philosophy.

When the judge at the Clayoquot trials called me "magnificently unrepentant" I really appreciated his remark. He was a wonderful fellow.

I considered my grandfather to be a very practical Christian who actually practised what he preached. It did not matter to him what nationality or what religion or what creed a person was. If that person needed some help, grandfather would help. If he needed advice, grandfather would give advice, and he would give it freely, gently, and convincingly.

Christianity meant something then. It wasn't just a phrase. You didn't pray on your knees on Sunday and prey on somebody else on Monday. Grandmother was the same way although her wisdom was sometimes overshadowed by Granddad's ability to put it in a more understandable way.

My pioneer neighbours here in Cedar ... I don't think there was a single one of them who wasn't a mentor in one direction or another. They gave good advice; they had humorous stories to tell that had a purpose in many cases. If they saw you doing something they didn't approve of they would tell you and always in a kindly way. They wouldn't necessarily bawl you out unless you had been very bad, and then they were stern. They pointed out that there were consequences to your acts. Every child needs and should have a mentor: someone they can look up to, someone who is doing an honest, sincere, and constructive job in this world.

I lived through the Great Depression. The world was arming Adolf Hitler in preparation for staging World War Two. There were a lot of very positive and very dynamic people all around irrespective of the cause they stood for. Some were very evil and some were very good, but they were excellent speakers: Churchill, Roosevelt, Hitler, Mussolini, the Emperor of Japan, and our own political leaders in Canada. You could listen to these people on the radio, and I listened to all of them. The world was gradually starting to come out of the Great Depression. The banks were trying to strangle the world by making high profits, and they did. To a large extent they promoted the Depression because they never made so much money at any other time in their past or present history. They simply squeezed everyone— including governments—and then they backed Hitler who was obviously the bad boy of the bunch.

At the same time I was listening to these people and getting ideas from all over the place, I was reading Socrates, Marcus Aurelius, Cicero, Lenin, Churchill, and Roosevelt—three ancient people I was really interested in and three current ones.

Then there were other mentors. When I came back from Powell River I went to work part-time for M.G. Hill at Yellow Point Lodge. He always needed something done and I was trying to build my own home and do things for myself too. M.G. Hill was a fascinating man to work with and to know. He had a philosophy towards the world in which he felt he wanted to be part of the world and be part of nature and be part of the whole universe, and at the same time, not destroy any of it. I absorbed many of his ideas. If he chose a site for a new cottage, he didn't take the tree down, he moved it enough to accommodate the tree.

In England I came under the indelible influence of Arthur Dower. He was chairman of the National Parks Board as well as a structural engineer. He and his family were Quakers with very good and practical concepts of live and let live. He was a delight to know and he passed on a lot of wisdom, which I was happy to absorb.

There were others along the way. Later on I met quite a few Aboriginal people like Simon Lucas and Chief Dan George. Their simple, straightforward philosophy and way of life has had a strong influence on the way I think and act. I've also become very interested in the philosophy and history of the Stolo Nation in the Fraser Valley and the wisdom and knowledge of one of their people, Steve

Point. He is their chief as well as an anthropologist and scientist. At present he is working on a history of the petroglyphs.

We have had some good people in Canada and we have had some bad ones. Unfortunately I feel that the bad ones often develop because they didn't have proper mentors. They didn't have people to point out the difference between right and wrong when they were young. This is why we have so many lousy politicians and bad business people; they are actually corrupt and you can't describe them as anything else. It all goes back to a lack of proper mentoring. I think I have been fortunate in avoiding that type of individual or I have been shown a way to avoid them.

I realize that even in this plastic, blindfolded age that stifles people's minds, there are people who stay out of that quagmire. We have had some good people - some good political people: M.J. Coldwell, Harold Winch, Warren Allman, and Pierre Trudeau in his own way. These people were far above the rank and file of the others. It is possible to find good in almost any situation and among any group of people. I feel there is hope for the world. We still have people fighting for the cause of good. At one point good will triumph over evil. How far away that point is, it's difficult to say.

In our society we like to say, "It's not possible. We can't afford it. We can't do it." Graham Towers, the first president of the Bank of Canada, said on being cross-examined on the role of finance in our society, that what is physically possible and socially desirable is financially feasible. In other words, we can finance good works.

There is hope. Bad situations usually develop good leaders. I believe we are at the point where we are about to develop those leaders, leaders who have values.

I am reminded of a quotation from Omar Khayyám. It is about the end of one thing and the beginning of something new:

Awake, for morning in the bowl of night
Has cast the stone that puts the stars to flight
And lo, that great hunter of the East
Has caught the Sultan's turret in a noose of light.

Merve Wilkinson receives his Order of British Columbia
from Lieutenant-Governor Garde Gardom.

In July 2001, just days after being awarded the Order of British
Columbia, Merve Wilkinson received word that he was to be invested
with the Order of Canada later that year. The Order of Canada is
the nation's highest honour.

Wilkinson was cited for his work with the Leadership Initiative
for Earth (LIFE) and also for his contributions over the years including the forming and running of the junior drama club in Yellow
Point, his involvement with the co-operative movement, and his
educational work with schools in Canada and other countries.

Musing on this the latest of many public honours to come his
way, Wilkinson said, "We've had about enough awards for this
century. They'll have to save some to award to some of my disciples
in the next century."

Index

Photo Credits

Nanaimo Daily News (p. 217, 230).

Nanaimo Museum (p. 26, 27, 29, 66)

Glen Olsen (p. 236)

Sunfire Publications Ltd. archives (p. 24)

Heritage House collection (p. 37)

The remainder of the photos have been provided by Goody Niosi or Merve Wilkinson.

Goody Niosi was born in Karlsruhe, Germany, in 1946. At five she immigrated to Canada and grew up in Ontario. She recalls learning to read intuitively and falling in love with books. At ten she promised herself she would be a writer when she grew up.

Goody didn't become a writer until she was 49. Her first career was in the film industry. She worked in Toronto and Vancouver as a film editor. She found time in her busy career to get married twice, to travel around the world once, and to explore Europe several times.

"What you do in your life gives you a partial picture of a person," Goody says. "To really know someone, ask them what their passions are.

"I am passionate about ideas and ideals. I am passionate about love and seeing the magic in everyday things. I am passionate about walking with my dog through dark and snowy woods while Robert Frost's words circle through my head. I am passionate about corny love songs. I am passionate about truth and justice and seeing people smile with their eyes and hearts.

"If I can do one thing in my writing, I hope to be able to make a difference. I hope to always be in love with love and to always see the miracles in a blade of grass, a seedling poking its head through the ground, an apple tree in springtime bloom."

Magnificently Unrepentant is Goody's first book and in the subject of eco-forester Merve Wilkinson she has found a man who had made a difference.

Goody writes for the *Nanaimo Daily News*, *Harbour City Star*, and other publications. She lives above a country stable with her two dogs. When she is not outdoors or involved in various community activities you will probably find her plunked down in front of her computer.